STEP BY STEP GARDENING

Series Editor
ALAN TITCHMARSH

Gardening for Beginners

Graham Rice

Ward Lock Limited · London

© Ward Lock Ltd 1985

First published in Great Britain in 1985
by Ward Lock Limited, 82 Gower Street,
London WC1E 6EQ, a Pentos Company.

House editor Denis Ingram
Designed by Bob Swan

Text filmset in Monophoto Plantin 110
by MS Filmsetting Limited,
Frome, Somerset

Printed and bound in Italy
by New Interlitho SpA, Milan

**British Library Cataloguing in
Publication Data**

Rice, Graham
    Gardening for beginners.—(Step-by-step
    Gardening Series)
    1. Gardening
    I. title   II. Series
    635   SB450.97

ISBN 0-7063-6266-7

CONTENTS

ACKNOWLEDGEMENTS

(Numbers in parentheses designate Figure numbers; letters in parentheses: t = top, m = middle, b = bottom, l = left, r = right)

All the line drawings are by Nils Solberg.

The drawings on pp. 8(1,3); 13(1); 14(1–3); 27(1–5); 30(1–3); 31(t3); 46(t & b); 57(t); 58(t & br); 59; 60(1); 64; 65(3, 4, 7 & 8), & 67(br) are after the illustrations on pp. 129; 132; 136; 52, 53; 155; 58; 154; 246; 60, 251; 251; 47; 34; 34; & 37 respectively in *Step-by-Step Gardening*, A. Wilbur, Willow Books/Collins, 1982.

The drawings on pp. 81(t); 83(tl, tr, m, br); 85(tl, tr, m); & 87(tl, m, br) are after the illustrations on pp. 20; 1, 28, 19, 5; 10, 11, 6; & 21, 30, 14 respectively in *Pests and Diseases Troubleshooter*, G. Culpan, Practical Gardening/Murphy Chemical 1983. The drawings on pp. 91(tl, tr, bl, br); 92(l. m. r); & 93(tl) are after the drawings on pp. 25, 83, 49, 95; 71, 85, 141; & 90 respectively in *The Need to Weed*, V. Ailes, Murphy Chemical Ltd., 1981.

The drawings on pp. 48(m, b) & 49 are after the drawings on pp. 40 & 56 respectively in *Pruning*, Graham Rice, Octopus, 1982. The drawing on p. 72 is after the drawing on p. 32 in *Gardening DIY*, D. Stevens, Octopus, 1982. The drawings on pp. 81(b); 85(bl); & 87(br) are after the drawings on pp. 53; 21; & 87 respectively in *Pestfree Plants*, A. Titchmarsh, Octopus, 1982.

The drawing on p. 45(m) is after the drawing on p. 22 in *Gardeners' World Vegetable Book*, G. Hamilton, British Broadcasting Corporation, 1981. The drawings on p. 21 are after the illustrations on p. 3 in *Hardy Bulbs – 2*, C. F. Coleman, Penguin, 1964. The drawing on p. 16 (l) is after the drawing on p. 26 in the *Hillier Good Gardening Guide*, D. Woodland, Hamlyn, 1978.

The drawings on pp. 6(2–5); 8(2); 9–11; 13(2–7); 15; 18; 19(b); 20(m, b); 30(t); 32–37; 40(b); 41–44; 45(t, b); 51(t); 53(b); 55; 57(m, b); 58(2, 3); 63; 67(1–3); 69–71; 74–77; 83(br); & 93(tr) are after photographs the copyright of which belong to *Practical Gardening* and *Amateur Gardening* magazines, B. Alfieri, R. Corbin, B. Furner, and Harry Smith Horticultural Photographic Collection.

The drawings on pp. 6(tl); 6(ml); 24(t); 24(b); 25(tl); 25(m); 25(bl); 25(r); 39; 46(m); 50; 51(m, b); & 78 are after illustrations appearing in promotional literature of Rotocrop Ltd.; Brackley Sawmills; Bulldog Tools; Plantpak Ltd.; Wolsey Webb Ltd.; McCullogh Ltd.; Flymo Ltd; Hayter plc; I & S Unwin; Fyba Ltd., Halls Homes & Hardens; Camplex; and Essex Products Ltd., respectively.

Publishers Note

Measurements are generally cited in imperial followed by the metric equivalent in parentheses. In a few instances, owing to pressure on space, the metric equivalent has been omitted.

It's exciting and yet it's daunting, starting a new garden. There's so much to do and so much to learn that the beginner is often put off making a start. Every book he opens is so crammed with information that the basic know-how becomes lost in a welter of detail. *Gardening For Beginners* avoids putting off the tyro by sticking to the simple essentials of gardening and demonstrating them clearly with step-by-step diagrams and a common-sense approach.

Graham Rice covers all the basic skills you'll need to turn your wilderness into a pleasure garden. Everything from clearing the site and cultivating the earth to choosing and buying plants and tools, setting up a greenhouse, starting from scratch with a lawn, growing plants indoors and dealing with pests, diseases and weeds.

When you've mastered the basic craft of gardening there are other books in the series to satisfy your specialist curiosity: *Greenhouse Gardening*, *Plant Propagation*, and that bane of the gardener's life, *Pruning*. These books are designed and written to help you get the most enjoyment out of your garden with the least amount of worry.

☼ Plastic compost bin with sliding panels.

3 Add layer of garden waste.

1 Wooden compost bin with removable front panels.

4 Water heap if dry.

2 Bricks in bottom help ventilation.

5 Sprinkle activator to speed up decomposition.

Making garden compost

1
SOIL AND CULTIVATIONS

Compost and organic matter
Good soil is the foundation of all good gardening. Unless your soil is looked after well, no matter what plants you put in and regardless of the fertilizers you spread, your plants will not thrive. **Soils** come in a wide variety of types – some are very sandy and some contain a lot of clay which makes them sticky. In almost all cases the way to improve them is to add organic matter. This is just a fancy name for muck, but also includes anything which is derived from plants or animals, however remotely – animal manures of all sorts, peat, garden compost plus other less commonly used materials such as spent mushroom compost, leaf mould and bark. When any of these items is added to dry, sandy soil the result is to prevent water running through quickly and the soil then stays moist for longer. On heavy soil it helps break up clay into smaller granules and keeps them from sticking together. Once added to the soil it slowly rots and as it does so plant foods are released into the soil.
Farmyard manure Although this is recommended strongly in all the old books, it is not vital. Riding stables are often the most convenient source, especially if reasonably small quantities are needed. Never use fresh manure; either buy it well rotted or stack it for six months before use. If it is applied fresh, the soil bacteria will use all the available nitrogen to rot it down – nitrogen that is needed by the plants.
Peat Very useful and easy to buy in the garden centre. If you can, buy a big bag as it will work out cheaper. The problem with peat is that it contains almost no plant food so you'll have to make sure you add fertilizer as well.
Garden compost This is the most economical source of organic matter as most of the constituents will come from your own garden and kitchen. It is not difficult to make and does not require much effort.

First of all you need something to keep all the materials together – a bin, box or bag.

☼ Ready made plastic bins are small enough to fit into an odd corner of the garden. Alternatively you can make your own out of scrap timber.

1 Old floorboards are ideal. These have the advantage of holding in the heat generated as the compost rots and the hotter the compost gets, the better it will be.

2 Having made your bin, put a few bricks on edge in the bottom to let in the air and then add a layer of twigs such as hedge clippings to stop all the weeds falling through.

3 Next comes a layer of compostable garden waste 6–9 in (15–23 cm) deep. You can use annual weeds (not perennial thick rooted kinds), any raw vegetable waste from the kitchen – potato peelings, cabbage leaves and the like – plus leaves and grass mowings.

Do not put in too much grass as it will not rot properly and try to mix it with other materials. Now sprinkle on something to help it all rot. Compost activator is ideal, or you can use a fertilizer such as sulphate of ammonia.

4 If the materials are dry soak the heap at this stage.

5 Carry on with 6–9 cm (15–23 in) layers of organic waste then a sprinkling of activator until you fill the bin. When you run out of material, or when the bin is full, cover the heap with an old piece of carpet to keep the worst of the rain out and the heat in.
Pulverized bark This comes in two forms – shredded and composted.

[1] Making the first trench.

[2] Adding compost to first trench.

[3] Making the second trench.

[4] Filling last trench of the half plot.

[5] Filling last trench of the whole plot.

Shredded bark is ideal as a weed suppressing mulch, particularly on beds of heathers and conifers. Composted bark, which usually has fertilizers added to give a balance of plant foods, is a good substitute for garden compost and is particularly valuable for use when planting trees and shrubs.

Other materials The contents of used growing bags are excellent and some commercial tomato growers sell off their old ones very cheaply; the same applies to mushroom growers and their old compost. Both are good buys.

Digging

The basic technique of soil cultivation is digging and this is also the simplest way of getting organic matter into the soil. Digging comes in two forms, single and double – the latter is twice as strenuous! Ordinary, or single digging involves turning and breaking up the soil and putting compost in.

Single digging

First of all divide the area to be dug in two parts lengthways by stretching a string between two canes.

[1] Dig a trench the depth of your spade and about 18 in (45 cm) wide across the end of half the plot putting

the soil at the same end of the other half. If you're piling it on grass put a sheet of polythene down first.

2 Now put a 2 in (5 cm) layer of compost or other organic material on the bottom of the trench.

3 Throw the soil from the undug part of the plot forward to cover the compost. Break it up with the edge of the spade and remove any white, fleshy, weed roots. Line the bottom of the newly created trench with compost and carry on down the plot until you get to the end. You will be left with an empty trench with compost in the bottom.

4 Fill this gap with soil from a new trench on the other side of the string and carry on working back down the plot until you arrive alongside the point where you started.

5 Fill the last trench with the soil from the first trench.

It's often said that the best time to dig is when you have the time but, ideally, if your soil is heavy and sticky dig in the autumn, otherwise in spring. And don't do too much at once. If you are not used to it, half an hour at a time with a half hour break will make sure you don't strain your back or your patience.

You will probably find that your plot looks rather uneven when you've finished, especially if you are not used to digging. Leave it to settle for a while (until spring if you dug in autumn) then roughly level it off with a spade or rake.

Double digging
Double digging takes more effort but is also more effective.

☼ The difference is that having dug your trench – and it helps to dig a wide one – you fork over the bottom to the full depth of the fork. Then put in the compost and fork it in. If your soil has

been dug in the recent past and compost added, instead of digging you can spread your compost over the surface and fork it into the top 9 in (23 cm) of soil.

In the area where you grow vegetables try to dig one third of the plot each year. In the garden, where you will probably plant shrubs and other permanent flowers, you cannot disturb the soil deeply so it's a good idea to 'mulch'. This odd word simply means spreading your compost or peat in a layer over the surface. It will rot down slowly, worms will take it into the soil and it will also help to suppress weeds and retain moisture. Spread your compost in the early spring when the soil is already moist.

In the autumn any remains can be forked lightly into the soil, but make sure you disturb no more than the top couple of inches otherwise you may damage the roots of your shrubs. Nowadays most gardeners prefer to leave their mulches in place all the year round. It saves both effort and money.

☼ Double digging.

Fertilizers and lime

The other important factors in the production of good soil and good plants are the levels of lime and plant food. Lime controls the degree of acidity or alkalinity of a soil. This is important because different plants prefer different amounts of lime. Although most garden plants are not too fussy about soil acidity, if your soil is very acid and grows good rhododendrons, you might have to add lime in order to grow some other plants well. Conversely, rhododendrons won't grow on a limy soil.

In order to find out how limy your soil is a soil test kit is very useful. This offers a simple chemical method of ascertaining the acidity or alkalinity of your soil and will tell you how much lime to add, if any.

1 Soil is collected from about 2 in (5 cm) down and left in a saucer to dry.

2 A little indicator fluid from the kit is put in the test tube supplied (there is a mark to show how much to put in) and a measured amount of soil added to the liquid.

3 The two are then shaken up and when the mixture has settled the colour of the liquid is compared with the coloured panels on the chart supplied with the kit. This will tell you how acid

Plants which like acid soil
Azaleas
Camellias
Heathers
Lily of the valley
Magnolia
Rhododendrons

Plants which like lime
Asparagus
Beans
Blackcurrant
Cabbage
Carnations
Cotoneaster
Forsythia
Large-flowered iris
Lilac
Rock rose
Viburnum

or limy your soil is. If it is not suitable for the plants you want to grow the leaflet with the kit will tell you how much lime to add.

Very limy soil cannot be made more acid in the long term, though the addition of flowers of sulphur has a short-term effect.

Fertilizers are vital to healthy plant growth. Garden compost and other organic matter provide some plant food but the supply will not be balanced and

2 Collecting soil sample.

2 Adding soil to indicator tube.

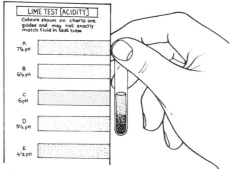

[3] Comparing tube liquid with pH chart.

there is unlikely to be enough unless you use large quantities.

There are three main plant foods: nitrogen, phosphates and potassium. Nitrogen encourages leafy growth and so is good for crops such as cabbage and lettuce and for lawns. Phosphates produce strong root growth so are used on crops like carrots and parsnips and to encourage new plants to make good root growth – this helps them settle in quickly. Potash encourages the production of flowers and helps produce good fruits, so it is used on fruit trees, flowering pot plants and crops such as tomatoes.

These rules are rather rough and ready and for general use a balanced fertilizer, such as growmore, which contains all three of these nutrients, is all you need. Although this will not produce the best results possible in all cases, it can be used safely on flower borders, fruit, vegetables and lawns. It comes in granules which are very easy to sprinkle at 2–4 oz (60–120 g) (one or two handfuls) per square yard (metre) depending on the state of your soil. Blood, bone and fishmeal is an organic fertilizer with similar properties to growmore, but it helps to feed the vital soil bacteria, too. If you want to use specific fertilizers, the main nitrogen-containing fertilizer is sulphate of ammonia; superphosphate is the main phosphate fertilizer, while for potash you should look for sulphate of potash.

There is a liquid formulation of growmore for the greenhouse and as a general feed for house plants, but specific house plants' feeds are available which are well worth using. Other specific feeds worth buying are those for tomatoes and for roses, which can be used on all flowering shrubs.

☼ Look out for these feeds in easy measure dispensers, which make it much simpler to measure out the correct amount.

☼ Making a liquid feed using an easy-measure dispenser.

Sowing seeds outside

The easiest way to grow new plants is to sow seeds and for many plants and most vegetables there is no other way. Annual flowers, perennial flowers and even trees and shrubs can be grown from seed and it is a cheap method which often requires little in the way of special equipment.

Vegetables and annual flowers are sown in the spot in which they will eventually mature so when deciding where to sow you should be guided by the requirements of the plant. You will usually find these on the seed packet. Biennials – plants which are sown one year, flower the next and then die, and trees, shrubs and herbaceous perennials which live for many years are usually sown in a seed bed and then transplanted to their permanent sites.

Your seed bed should be neither in full sun nor total shade all day. Sites for annuals and vegetables should be well prepared by digging but for seed beds just fork over and remove any weeds.

[1] After preparation the area should be trod to make sure it is firm. This is done by shuffling over the area putting your weight on your heels so that when you've finished you can see the rows of heel marks next to each other. Don't do this after recent rain.

The area should then be levelled with a garden rake. Any stones and large twigs should be removed and the soil broken down into small particles, so that the tiny roots the seed first produces will be able to get in contact with the soil quickly. Do not over-rake; dust-fine soil will cake in the first shower of rain.

Next some fertilizer is needed. The ideal fertilizer for seeds is superphosphate which encourages a strong root system – vital to the long term fortunes of the plants. However, growmore at the rate of a handful to every two square yards on seed beds, and a handful per square yard for vegetables and annuals, will give them a good start.

[2] Rake the soil again after spreading fertilizer.

All seeds are best sown in lines. This makes it easier to decide which are weeds. It also makes hoeing easier. For long rows a garden line is very useful. This can consist simply of nylon twine wound on to two short sticks.

[3] Use a cane or the edge of the rake or hoe to make shallow trenches (drills) in which to sow the seeds.

The theory is that seeds should be sown at twice their own depth but if you can make your drill about $\frac{1}{4}$ in (6 mm) deep for small seeds, $\frac{1}{2}$ in (13 mm) deep for larger ones and even deeper for big seeds like peas and beans they will usually do very well. Try and sprinkle small seeds in the drills as thinly as possible so that they rest $\frac{1}{4}$–$\frac{1}{2}$ in (6–12 mm) apart. Don't try to sow all the seeds in the packet.

[4] You can either tap the seeds from the packet with your finger or take pinches in your hand and sprinkle them from your fingers.

[5] Cover the seeds with a little soil from each side of the drill.

[6] Tap the soil over seeds gently with the back of the rake.

When it seems as if most of the seedlings have come up, many of them must be removed! The seed packet will tell you the final spacings but in the first instance thin to half these distances. Do this when the soil is moist.

[7] Put your fingers on either side of the plants you want to keep and then either pull up or hoe off the others.

Seed sowing

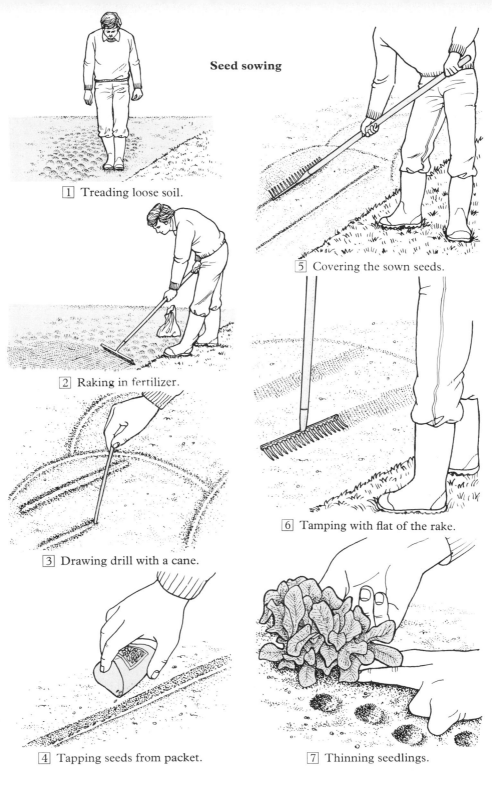

1 Treading loose soil.

2 Raking in fertilizer.

3 Drawing drill with a cane.

4 Tapping seeds from packet.

5 Covering the sown seeds.

6 Tamping with flat of the rake.

7 Thinning seedlings.

[1] Watering the young plants.

[2] Gently lifting a plant.

[3] Replanting in new position.

Transplanting

Some vegetables such as cauliflowers, cabbages, sprouts, broccoli and leeks, plus biennial plants like wallflowers, forget-me-nots and daisies have to be transplanted from their seed beds to the part of the garden where they are to reach maturity. It is important to transplant them in such a way that the shock is not too great.

[1] Firstly, the rows should be well watered if it has not rained in the previous 24 hours.

[2] Then, using a handfork for small plants and a digging fork for larger ones, gently lift the plants out keeping as much soil on the roots as possible. If you have only a few plants you can dig them up individually with a trowel. Your seed packet will give you final planting distances and a planting board marked with a double shallow saw cut every foot and a single cut every 3 in is useful. Another guideline is the use of your boot, which is about 1 ft (30 cm) long, and your trowel which is usually about 9 in (23 cm) long.

[3] Plant with a trowel, making sure that the plant is at the same depth in the soil as it was in its seed bed. Firm it with the handle of the trowel or using your fingers and thumb, then water it in well.

Larger plants can also be transplanted if necessary. Shrubs and trees which lose their leaves in the winter (deciduous) are best moved either just after their leaves have fallen or just before they start to appear. Evergreens are best moved in early autumn or mid to late spring. In all cases, but especially with evergreens, it is important to take as much root as possible and to keep as much soil on the roots as you can. It is often a waste of time trying to move anything larger than 6 ft (1.8 m), especially evergreens and conifers, but if larger plants have to be moved it helps to make a slit 1–1½ ft (30–45 cm) from the stem with a spade all round the plant six months before you move it. This will encourage more roots to grow nearer the stem.

Other cultivations

☼ Most of the other basic soil cultivation techniques are concerned with weeds, in particular hoeing. The blade of the Dutch hoe slices very shallowly through the soil, loosening tiny weed seedlings and cutting off slightly larger ones. These are left to die on the surface of the soil unless there are large numbers of them. It is best to hoe on a sunny day so that weeds dry out and die before they have any chance to take root again. Unfortunately if it rains soon after hoeing much of your good work may be undone.

Ideally, you should hoe regularly, say every week, whether you can see weeds or not. That way even the tiniest seedlings on the point of emerging will be prevented from establishing themselves.

Be very careful to avoid damaging plants when you hoe. It's easy to catch the edge of a stem and any wounds will set back the plant and let in diseases.

Large numbers of small weeds can be removed by hoeing but larger weeds need different treatment. A fork is the best tool.

✿ If you find any white stringy roots running out into the soil or thick, thong-like ones going deep down, try not to break them off but follow them along to the very end and remove them completely. Many of these roots are so prolific that even the smallest portion left or broken off will grow into a new weed.

☼ Hoeing between rows of lettuces.

✿ Using fork to extricate weed root.

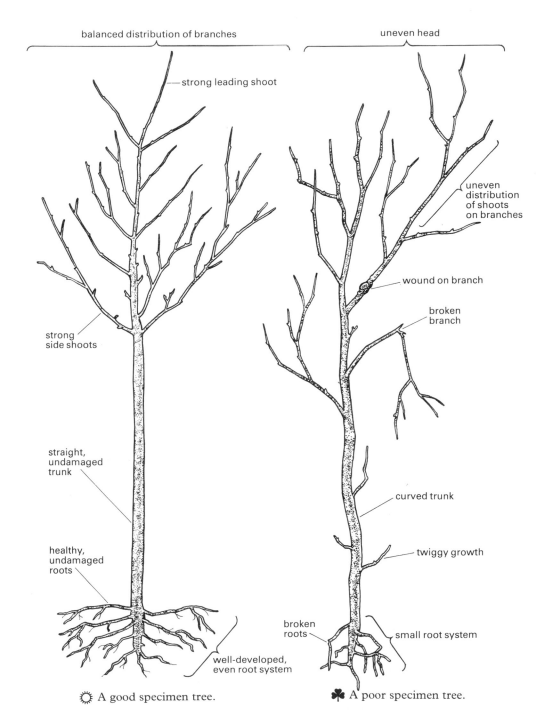

balanced distribution of branches

uneven head

strong leading shoot

uneven distribution of shoots on branches

strong side shoots

wound on branch

broken branch

straight, undamaged trunk

curved trunk

healthy, undamaged roots

twiggy growth

broken roots

small root system

well-developed, even root system

☼ A good specimen tree.

☘ A poor specimen tree.

2
BUYING PLANTS AND EQUIPMENT

Introduction

Visiting a garden centre can be a bewildering experience if you are coming to gardening for the first time. All those rows of plants and shelves of chemicals are very off putting. The first thing to do if you're in doubt about what to buy is to ask for help. If you explain exactly what you want the staff will do their best to satisfy you. Value for money should really be the key and there are many ways in which you can make your money go further:

1 Buy small plants rather than large ones. Once planted they will grow quickly and the gaps can always be filled with cheaper, temporary plants.

2 Buy materials in large quantities if you can; it will usually work out cheaper. Co-operate with a friend or two if your needs are small.

3 Investigate any special offers but treat them with scepticism. Sometimes garden centres sell off surplus stock cheaply when it's too late in the season to use it.

4 Don't neglect markets, WI stalls and school fetes as sources of good bargains.

5 Remember that with tools and equipment in particular you get what you pay for and it's worth saving your money for something that will last.

6 Club together with a neighbour to buy boxes of bedding plants so that you get a wide variety without wasting any.

7 Make sure that plants you buy are free of pests, diseases and weeds – you don't want to introduce them into your own garden. If a plant looks below par, don't buy it.

8 Make sure when buying tools, and especially equipment, that they do what you want them to do.

9 Look in papers and magazines for special offers, but don't be tempted to buy things you don't need, and avoid buying plants which are advertised with over-enthusiastic descriptions accompanied by artists' impressions.

Trees

In an ideal world it is the trees, if there are to be any, which should be planted first in a garden. They are going to be the largest features but will also be the most expensive to buy. Small gardens may only have space for one tree but as they are so crucial to the pocket and the garden scene it is advisable not only to choose the variety carefully (p. 26) but also to choose a good specimen. This ensures that your tree establishes itself well and grows into a shapely plant.

☼ ♣ The drawings show a good and a poor specimen. Try to ensure your purchase has none of the defects shown in the poor specimen.

Garden centres sell trees in three ways. They may be grown in containers, they may have bare roots or they may have been dug up with soil on the roots and wrapped in hessian or plastic mesh.

Trees with bare roots are usually deciduous types and should only be bought while they remain leafless. Plant them straight away. Those with wrapped roots may be deciduous or evergreen. Evergreens should be bought and planted in spring or autumn, deciduous types while they are leafless. Trees grown in pots and other containers may be bought and planted at any time.

Shrubs

Shrubs almost invariably come pot-grown in containers (usually thin, black polythene bags), though some have their roots wrapped in hessian. Container-grown shrubs can be planted at any time of year while root-wrapped ones should only go in when they are not growing. I would always recommend container-grown types. You can then see the plants in flower at the garden centre or nursery, pick the ones you like and put them in the garden straight away.

A guarantee of quality, which is worth looking out for, is the 'Gardener's Best' label. This label is only to be found on plants which have been carefully inspected and found to achieve a very high standard, higher than the British Standard for shrubs.

☼♣ Again it's important to assess critically your potential purchase – make sure your plant has the qualities of the good specimen illustrated and not the defects of the poor specimen.

Border plants

Buying border plants is a little more tricky than buying shrubs. Border plants, also called herbaceous plants, die down in the winter so there is nothing to see at that time of year to give you a clue as to the quality.

♧ Border plants, and also rock plants, may be pot or container grown, they may have their roots wrapped in polythene, or come packed in peat in a polythene bag.

✻ If you get them through the post they may be shrink wrapped in polythene or be wrapped in newspaper.

Some plants, like chrysanthemums and carnations bought by mail order may come with bare roots, though they will probably have some soil clinging to

☼ A good specimen shrub.

♣ A poor specimen shrub.

them and be wrapped in shavings. These are often very sturdy little plants although with so little soil they do look vulnerable. It's important to put them into pots and to grow them on the windowsill or in a greenhouse, before putting them out in the garden.

If you buy in a garden centre, buy in the spring and you will then at least be able to see that the plants are growing and how many shoots they have. If you buy by mail order, go to a reliable supplier, preferably one recommended by a friend or in a magazine. If you are not satisfied complain.

◊ Bedding plants are also sold in many ways. The most well-established plants, which are also the most expensive, are in single pots, but the next best – and more reasonably priced – are those sold in compartmentalized trays. Most bedding plants are fairly resilient and even the old method where the stall holder on the market cuts them out of the wooden tray with a knife still produces good plants in the garden.

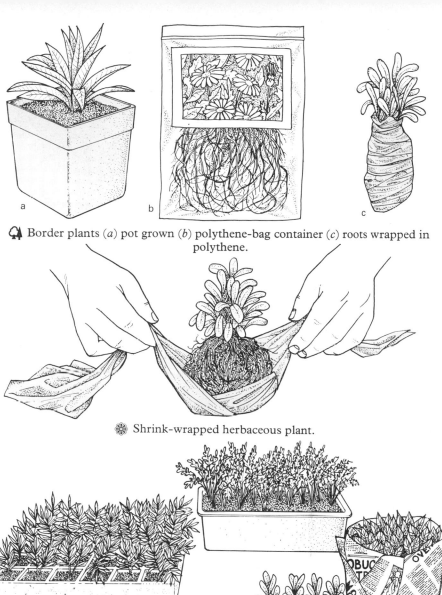

🌲 Border plants (*a*) pot grown (*b*) polythene-bag container (*c*) roots wrapped in polythene.

❀ Shrink-wrapped herbaceous plant.

⟡ Bedding plants are sold in various packs.

☼ Airtight, foil-seed packet.

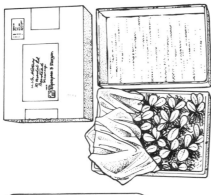

✿ Two types of container used for transit of seedlings and young plants.

Seeds

Buying seeds is by no means as problematical as it once was. The information given on the seed packets and in the catalogues is comprehensive, and the colour pictures show you, albeit rather enthusiastically, what you will get when your seeds mature. The actual seeds you buy have been tested for quality too – they should be guaranteed to come up under favourable conditions, and should certainly be what the packet says they are.

☼ You will find many seeds in foil packets. These are a little more expensive but the airtight sachets protect the seeds from moisture in the air which otherwise quickly causes them to deteriorate. All the seeds will produce good results if you follow the directions on the packet, but you will still find apparently similar types on sale at widely varying prices. The cheap varieties will give you good crops and good flowers and initially I should stick to them. If they should fail you won't have lost too much and when they succeed you'll still be well pleased. More expensive types give superb results but are often more difficult to germinate.

Some varieties, especially those such as petunias with very small, expensive seeds, are available as pelleted seed. Each seed is enclosed in a round pellet of dried clay which is much easier to handle than the seed itself. When sown in moist soil, the pellet crumbles and the seed germinates. (If pelleted seed is sown in dry soil, the pellet does not crumble and the seed will not come up.)

✿ Mail order seed companies now sell seedlings and young plants of the more difficult varieties. This is an expensive way of buying plants but very useful for the beginner with no special facilities.

Bulbs

Bulbs represent a prime case where buying cheap can be a waste of money, or worse. Many of the bulbs you find sold cheaply at markets, or even at roadsides, are cheap because they are diseased. Some bulb diseases are very difficult to eradicate so avoid bulbs that appear to be exceptional bargains. Also beware bulbs which are sold at a reduced rate late in, or even after the planting season. Many of these will be slightly shrivelled and will probably have long shoots already growing from the tips. Results from these bulbs are very unpredictable although they will always flower later than bulbs planted at the right time.

The most economic way of buying bulbs is to buy them loose. You'll find most garden centres will have boxes of loose bulbs with a colour picture to show what you're getting and bags to fill with as many as you need. This is better value than buying pre-packed bulbs.

🌳 Some bulbs come in a variety of sizes at different prices. Round bulbs will produce one flower, double nosed will produce two, while offsets will probably not flower at all in their first year but will in the year after planting. Always choose bulbs which are plump and firm.

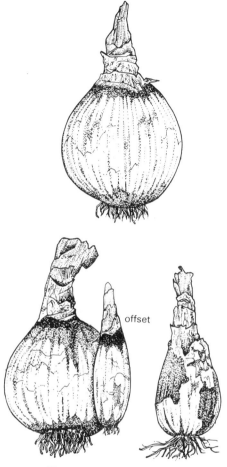

offset

🌳 Some typical bulb shapes.

Type	Planting depth		Planting distance		Planting time
	in	(cm)	in	(cm)	
Spring flowering bulbs					
Daffodils	6	(15)	5–6	(12.5–15)	Early autumn
Crocus	3	(7.5)	3	(7.5)	Autumn
Snowdrops	3	(7.5)	3	(7.5)	Early autumn
Tulips	4	(10)	5–6	(12.5–15)	Autumn
Summer flowering bulbs					
Gladioli	5	(12.5)	6	(15)	Spring
Lilies	6	(15)	12	(30)	Spring

House plants

As with so many other things, finding good buys in house plants entails going to a good supplier. Good garden centres and chain stores are the places to look and the places to avoid are markets and greengrocers' shops. House plants are raised in the protected environment of a greenhouse so any that are outside on a pavement or stall should be left alone. The shock of the wide world will set them back badly.

For an impressive effect as soon as possible after buying look for plants which are shapely and bushy. Some, like rubber plants, look better with one tall, majestic stem.

☼ However, ivies, for example, can be found as one long straggling shoot or as neat plants with three or four short shoots. The latter will give you better plants more quickly. Parasol plants are often grown with two or three separate plants in one pot. These, too, give a very substantial effect quickly. It is also possible to split them into three and pot them up separately, but you risk losing them and I would only attempt the operation in spring or summer if you have a greenhouse.

Avoid buying plants that are pre-wrapped; you can't see if there are any pests or diseases present, and also avoid buying any with yellowing leaves. Try and get the shop to wrap your plants for you as exposure to cold winds can damage delicate foliage and flowers. Don't put them in the boot of the car which can get very cold; keep them inside.

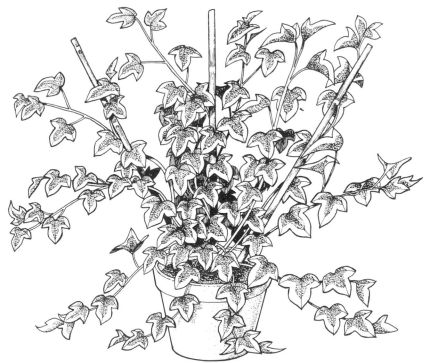

☼ Use of three canes to support a prolific ivy house plant.

Chemicals

There is a wide range of chemicals on the market both for feeding plants and killing pests, diseases and weeds. Fertilizers were dealt with on p. 10. When it comes to pesticides the best plan is to buy a general insecticide and general fungicide. Weedkillers tend to have more specialist uses and so it's better to buy the product for the particular job in hand (p. 90). Brand names change each year but a range of general insecticides on the market includes Bio Long-last, Murphy Tumblebug and ICI Sybol 2.

There are rather fewer fungus diseases to trouble your plants and a general fungicide will take care of most of them. Examples of fungicides: pbi Benlate, May and Baker Fungus Fighter and Murphy Tumbleblite.

It is also wise to buy in relatively small quantities. This is inevitably an expensive way of buying but it avoids the problem of having half-used bottles hanging around for long periods with the resultant deterioration and danger to children and animals.

♣ Powder or granular types are increasingly finding their way on to the market and these should be used whenever possible. They are packed in measured sachets so there is no awkward measuring and can be bought to make up the relatively small quantities that are often needed.

Weedkillers come in a variety of types. Some will burn off the foliage, others will kill roots too, some will kill grass weeds and not grass while yet others prevent weeds coming up but don't kill them once they're growing. Again, try and buy weedkillers in sachets or easy measure dispensers as this avoids all the bother of fiddly measuring into tablespoons and bottle caps. More details on p. 90.

♣ Use powdered chemicals, packed in measured sachets, wherever possible.

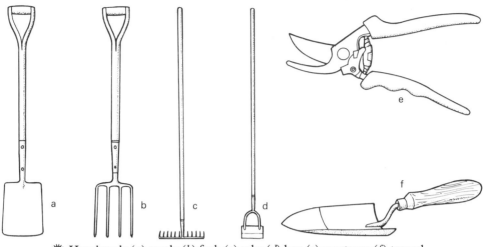

☼ Hand tools (*a*) spade (*b*) fork (*c*) rake (*d*) hoe (*e*) secateurs (*f*) trowel.

Hand tools

☼ Hand tools are amongst the most expensive items for the new gardener. Fortunately there are really only six items which are essential: spade, fork, rake, hoe, secateurs and trowel. Being realistic, to buy even these tools in the best quality is going to be expensive; because the rake and hoe will get less heavy work and probably be used less often, second-best quality will probably suffice here. But for new gardeners with a garden in need of preparation, a good fork and spade are worthwhile investments – they will be regularly used and should last almost a lifetime. Cheap trowels are a waste of money, quite simply because they bend, especially in heavy soil.

Other items which are useful include a garden line – at its simplest a length of polypropylene twine between two short canes, marker board (p. 14), dibber, twine, watering can, plus a range of pots and trays for raising seedlings and for pot plants ♣.

♣ Typical range of plastic pots and trays used for raising seedlings and pot plants.

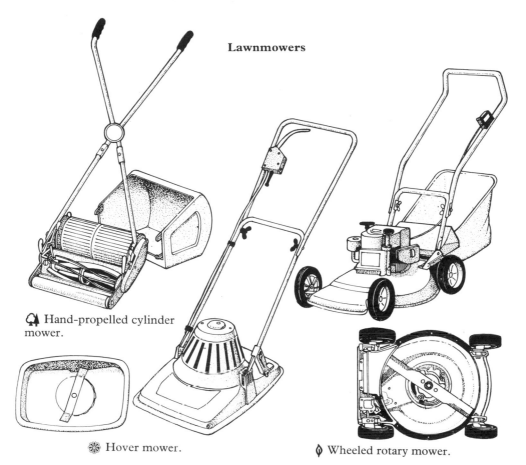

Hand-propelled cylinder mower.

Hover mower.

Wheeled rotary mower.

Lawn mowers

Everyone with grass needs a lawn-mower. There are three main types and three sources of power.

The traditional type is the cylinder mower with a rotating cylinder of blades which cuts against a fixed blade rather like a pair of scissors.

Hover mowers float over the grass on a cushion of air and a blade rotates horizontally to cut the grass.

Wheeled rotary mowers are similar to hover mowers but they are mounted on wheels rather than supported on an air cushion.

Power is available from electricity, petrol or the operator's own efforts.

For small gardens, electric machines (either hover or cylinder) are ideal and the choice is largely a matter of personal preference. If you like stripes you must choose a cylinder mower but if you have plants close to the edge of the grass, choose a hover – it won't damage them. In both cases only the blades are powered; you still have to push the machine. For large gardens, especially if there is some rougher grass, wheeled rotaries are more suitable, particularly those with powered wheels; they require little effort to use. There is a lot of competitive price cutting in mowers so it's a good plan to shop around as much as possible for the best deal. Second-hand mowers, especially small electric ones, can be very risky buys and with the prices of new machines so reasonable, they represent a gamble.

3
ORNAMENTAL PLANTS

Trees

Great care is needed when choosing trees, especially for the small garden. Many trees look handsome when they are small, grow very quickly and then begin to get out of hand. The answer is to choose wisely in the first place and so avoid the problems of too much shade, hungry roots and too many leaves.

Trees for small gardens

Cherries The variety 'Amanogawa' is tall and narrow and casts little shade. The flowers are pale pink and scented.
Birch Choose the dwarf type, *Betula pendula* 'Youngii' known as Young's Weeping Birch. It takes up the least space and is very elegant.
Conifers Many conifers are suitable but avoid Leyland Cypress which gets enormous, and plain Lawson cypress which is dull and oppressive.
Maple The coral bark maple (*Acer palmatum* 'Senkaki') is a delicate small tree with red twigs and fingered leaves that turn golden in autumn.
Laburnum Choose only the variety 'Vossii' which has the largest flowers and is without the poisonous seeds of other types.

Planting a tree properly is very important. It will be there for many years so it is vital to give it a good start. Firstly, decide where it is to go. Don't plant it too near the house where it will shade the windows and don't put it in the middle of the lawn – this gives a dull, formal appearance to the garden and most of it will be shaded. Secondly, if your tree is a container-grown one, water it a couple of hours before planting.

[1] It's best to dig a large hole about 2½ ft (75 cm) across, and if you're planting on grass, heap the soil on a poly-thene sheet. Make the hole about the depth of your space.

[2] Next, fork in some organic matter, such as a mixture of peat and bonemeal, into the bottom of the hole and firm it with your foot. Stand the tree in the hole and knock in the stake on the windward side. [3] The wind will then blow the tree away from the stake and it won't rub the bark.

[4] Lay a cane or the rake handle across the hole and add or remove soil so that the top of the compost in the container (or the soil mark on the trunk of a bare-root tree) is about 2 in (5 cm) below the level of the surrounding soil. Take the plant out of its container and sit it in position.

[5] Mix some peat with the soil from the hole and refill in stages firming with the toe of your boot as you go. Keep filling until the soil is just above the root ball or the tree roots. This will leave a hollow which will collect rain and make watering easier.

Lastly tie the tree to the stake with a proprietary tree tie. Water in well, putting a little liquid feed in the water if you have it.

It's important to keep the soil well moistened especially if you plant in the summer. You'll probably find that the soil that was in the pot will dry out more quickly so the area around the stem will need more water. If the shape of the tree is slightly uneven or if any branches have been broken during planting trim them up with secateurs. Similarly, any broken roots should be cut off bare-root trees before they are planted.

Tree planting

[1] Digging the planting hole.

[2] Fork in peat/bonemeal mixture.

[4] Positioning the tree in the hole.

[3] Knock in stake.

[5] Refill the hole, firming as you go.

Shrubs (H = height: S = spread)

Shrubs for spring

Forsythia Spring shrub with yellow flowers which is tremendous value. 'Lynwood' is the best variety. H 6 ft (1.8 m); S 6 ft.

Flowering currant (*Ribes*) Dramatic spring shrub with red, pink or white flowers; very easy to grow. H 8 ft (2.4 m); S 4 ft (1.2 m).

Rhododendron Spring-flowering evergreens with a wide range of flower colours and sizes. An acid soil (p. 10) is essential.

Magnolia Exotic looking shrubs with small starry white flowers (*Magnolia stellata*) H 4 ft (1.2 m); S 4 ft or larger cup shaped flowers that are white or white flushed maroon (*Magnolia soulangiana*) H 8 ft (2.4 m); S 6 ft (1.8 m).

Japonica (*Chaenomales*) Apple-blossom shaped flowers in red, pink or white. Best trained against a wall or fence. Little or no pruning needed. H 4 ft (1.2 m); S 5 ft (1.5 m).

Shrubs for summer

Butterfly Bush (*Buddleia davidii*) Easy shrubs with long plumes of purple, lilac or white flowers. Attracts butterflies. H 5 ft (1.5 m); S 4 ft (1.2 m) if pruned each spring.

Rose of Sharon (*Hypericum*) Two types; one (*Hypericum calycinum*) grows to 1 ft (30 cm) and creeps, the other *Hypercium* 'Hidcote' is larger and bushier, H 5 ft (1.5 m); S 4 ft (1.2 m). Both have large butter-yellow flowers for many weeks.

Roses Wide variety of sizes and colours including valuable climbers. No need to grow them in a bed of their own.

Veronica (*Hebe*) Long-flowering evergreens with flowers in reds, blues, purples and white. H 4 ft (1.2 m); S 4 ft.

Hydrangea Tough shrubs with pink or blue flowers according to soil – pink on chalky soils, blue on acid ones. A colorant can be bought from a garden centre and used to turn some pink varieties blue. H 4 ft (1.2 m); S 4 ft.

Shrubs for autumn

Fuchsia Only a few varieties can be left outside all the year round. All varieties can go outside for the summer. H 2½ ft (75 cm); S 2½ ft (75 cm).

Californian lilac (*Ceanothus*) Delightful powder-blue flowers, good on summy walls. 'Gloire de Versailles' is an excellent variety. H 6 ft (1.8 m); S 5 ft (1.5 m).

Tree hollyhock (*Hibiscus*) White, pink or blue flowers that look very exotic. Neat and slow growing at first but eventually quite large. H 5 ft (1.5 m); S 4 ft (1.2 m).

Firethorn (*Pyracantha*) White flowers in early summer and a very impressive display of red, orange or yellow berries in autumn. A good wall shrub. H 8 ft (2.4 m); S 6 ft (1.8 m).

Cotoneaster A wide variety of shapes and sizes according to type but all have bright scarlet berries. *Cotoneaster horizontalis* is flat and spreading. H 2 ft (60 m); S 5 ft (1.6 m), *Cotoneaster* 'Cornubria' is tall and vigorous. H 10 ft (3 m); S 8 ft (2.4 m).

Shrubs for winter

Heathers (*Erica*) Red, pink or white bell flowers on bushy little plants. The only heaths happy in any soil are *Erica carnea*, H 9 in (23 cm); S 15 in (38 cm); *E. × darlyensis* H 1½ ft (45 cm); S 1½ ft and *E. mediterranea* H 2½ ft (75 cm); S 2 ft (60 cm). Others need lime-free soil.

Witch hazel (*Hamamelis*) Strongly

scented spidery flowers of bright yellow on bare twigs. Gold leaves in autumn too. H 5 ft (1.5 m); S 4 ft (1.2 m).

Laurustinus (*Viburnum tinus*) Evergreen with white flowers on and off all winter. Sometimes produces black berries later. H 8 ft (2.4 m); S 6 ft (1.8 m). The variety *Viburnum tinus* 'Eve Price' is more compact.

Daphne (*Daphne mezereum*) Small compact plant with pink or white flowers plus a strong scent. Slow growing. H 2½ ft (75 cm); S 2½ ft (75 cm).

Mahonia (*Mahonia japonica*) Tall plant with impressive leaves and long strings of bright yellow flowers. H 6 ft (1.8 m); S 5 ft (1.5 m).

Attractive evergreens

Conifers Enormous variety of shapes and sizes with foliage in green, blue, grey and gold. Look well with heathers. *Chamaecyparis pisifera* 'Boulevard' has silvery blue foliage. H 3 ft (90 cm); S 3 ft (90 cm). *Thuya occidentalis* 'Rheingold' is an invaluable variety with golden leaves. H 3 ft (90 cm); S 2½ ft (75 cm).

Elaeagnus The variety *Elaeagnus pungens* 'Maculata' is probably the finest of all variegated evergreens with big yellow splashes on the leaves. H 4 ft (1.2 m); S 5 ft (1.8 m).

Euonymus Wide variety of shapes and sizes with either silver or gold marking. All are good in the shade and some climb. *Euonymus fortunei* 'Emerald 'n' Gold' makes a spreading hummock of golden variegated leaves. H 1½ ft (45 cm); S 2 ft (60 cm). *E. fortunei* 'Silver Queen' has a creamy variegation and may climb. H 1 ft (30 cm); S 3 ft (90 cm).

Hollies (*Ilex*) Vigorous plants with plain leaves or in some varieties with bright edgings in gold, yellow or white. Berries in winter. *Ilex × alta clarensis* 'Golden King' H 6 ft (1.8 m); S 4 ft (1.2 m) has golden variegated leaves and berries well but plant *I. aquifolium* 'Golden Queen' as well to ensure a good crop of berries. H 5 ft (1.5 m); S 4 ft (1.2 m).

Ivies (*Hedera*) Good self-clinging climbers for shady walls. Leaves marked with gold, yellow, grey or white. Try *Hedera helix* 'Goldheart', H 8 ft (2.4 m); S 6 ft (1.8 m), which has small leaves. *H. canariensis* 'Variegata', H 12 ft (3.5 m); S 12 ft (3.5 m), is more vigorous, has a silvery edge to the leaf and is tender in the north.

Shrubs form the backbone of any garden and the choice is vast; it is hoped that the suggestions here will help you get started.

Growing shrubs

Planting is much the same as for trees.

Make sure you water the plant well and remove the polythene pot before planting, but don't disturb the roots too much. Don't firm the soil too hard, use your toe rather than the heel.

If you're planting in summer, plants may need watering every few days in hot weather until it is evident that they are established.

Pruning is often a problem but it can be reduced to a few simple rules. Plants like roses which flower in the summer are pruned as they start to grow in the spring – most of the previous years growth is removed.

Plants like forsythia (which flower in the spring on the shoots which grew the year before) are pruned by removing as much as possible of the shoots which have flowered. Do this as soon as the flowers fade.

☼ Layering by pegging down a shoot.

1 Taking cutting from deciduous shrub.

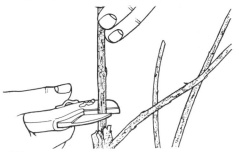

2 Trim cutting to 9 in (23 cm).

3 Set cuttings in a 6 in (15 cm) deep slit.

☼ Many shrubs are quite easy to increase. Low branches can be pegged down to the soil with hoops of wire and these will root in about a year when they can be cut off, dug up and replanted elsewhere. This type of propagation is known as layering.

1 2 3 Deciduous shrubs can also be rooted outdoors from cuttings. These are taken from the plant in early winter, trimmed to about 9 in (23 cm), dipped in rooting powder, and set about 4 in (10 cm) apart in a 6-in (15 cm) deep slit made with a spade.

Hedges

Hedges can be either a joy or a chore but by choosing the right plants and preparing the site well you can make a practical and attractive boundary. The planting method is a variation on normal shrub planting.

1 First dig a trench 18 in (45 cm) wide and one spit (spade blade) deep along the line of where the hedge is to go and heap the soil on polythene along one side. Fork over the bottom and add some organic matter such as garden compost or peat and bonemeal. Mix some organic matter with the soil from the trench and refill, firming well. Run a garden line along the trench exactly where the hedge is to run and then set the plants out at the appropriate distances apart.

2 Dig a hole just big enough for each plant, put it in and firm well with the toe then water in well. Cut back the plants by about a third to encourage bushiness. ♣ Conifers should not be cut back, but tied to a cane.

Mature hedges should be cut as often as necessary according to the vigour of the plants. Yew and cypress need only one trim a season, privet may need two or three. ♣ Always trim with the top slightly narrower than the bottom. Trim hedges with large leaves using secateurs; shears or powered trimmers are best for small-leaved hedges.

Plants for hedges

Privet (*Ligustrum*) Cheap, vigorous and easy to grow but needs frequent clipping and has hungry roots. Green and golden-leaved varieties. Plant 15 in (38 cm) apart.

Leyland's cypress (× *Cupressocyparis leylandii*) Very quick growing but not easy to keep to a reasonable size. Green- and yellow-leaved types available. H 30 ft (9 m) if unclipped. Plant 2½ ft (80 cm) apart. Clip in spring and summer, using secateurs at first.

Beech (*Fagus*) Tough and only needs clipping once a year. Keeps its old leaves all winter. Plant 18 in (45 cm) apart and trim each summer.

Roses Bush roses make splendid informal flowering hedges. Prune in spring. Try 'Queen Elizabeth' with scented pink flowers, H 5 ft (1.5 m), plant 2¼ ft (75 cm) apart. The white flowered 'Iceberg', H 3 ft (90 cm), is more bushy. Plant 2½ ft (75 cm) apart.

Western red cedar (*Thuya plicata*) A good evergreen hedge that is easy to keep to the right size.

Yew (*Taxus*) The best of all evergreens for hedging though slow to start. Best in a well-drained soil. Plant 1½ ft (45 cm) apart, and trim in summer.

Berberis There are evergreen and deciduous types. *Berberis stenophylla*, H 6 ft (1.8 m), is very spiny evergreen with yellow flowers in June. Plant 2 ft (60 cm) apart and trim immediately after flowering. The purple-leaved *Berberis thunbergii* 'Atropurpurea', H 5 ft (1.5 m), is deciduous and the leaves turn red in autumn. Plant 2 ft (60 cm) apart and trim in spring.

1 Digging trench for hedge planting.

2 Planting the young hedge plant.

Tying conifer plant to cane.

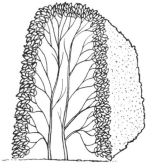

The ideal profile for a trimmed hedge.

Border plants

Border or herbaceous plants are those which die down to the ground, more or less, every winter but which come up again each spring. Few flower in the winter but they are amongst the easiest and most colourful of all plants for the rest of the year. There are varieties to suit every situation in the garden and the care they require is not great. Plant them from pots at any time of the year, although spring is probably most convenient, and apart from checking for pests and diseases the most important care they need is staking. Some, like Delphiniums, may reach as much as 6 ft (1.8 m) high and these are best staked using a single bamboo cane to each flower stem and tying with soft string.

☼ Shorter kinds are best supported with pea sticks, bushy twigs of hazel or birch, around the edge of the plant and looped round with string.

☼ Supporting border plants with canes and twine.

Dividing border plants

Many border plants increase their size fairly quickly and every three or four years it helps them if the clumps are divided. The central area, usually the oldest part of the plant, gets weak and can be thrown away. The vigorous growth at the edges can then be re-planted. There are usually enough shoots for a few pieces to be given to neighbours as well. Dividing is best done in autumn or spring.

1 Lift the plant with a fork and shake some of the soil off the roots.

2 Divide the clump either by manipulating two forks back to back or by slicing with a spade.

3 Alternatively the clump can be pulled apart by hand to make pieces with two or three strong shoots.

4 The site can then be improved by forking in some peat and a little fertilizer and the pieces re-planted.

5 In the autumn when the shoots have died back all the old dead stems can be cut down and used at the base of the compost heap although they are tough and may take a while to rot down.

Border plants for sunny spots

Flags (*Iris*) Stately plants flowering in early summer in many exotic shades. Divide after flowering. Staking not necessary. H 2–3 ft (60–90 cm); S 1 ft.

Delphiniums Blue, purple, pink or white flower spikes in summer. Most need staking. Slugs are fond of the young shoots. H 3–6 ft (90 cm–1.8 m); S 3 ft (90 cm).

Lupins Many single colours and bi-colours in early summer. Cut down immediately after flowering for more flowers later. H 2–4 ft (60 cm–1.2 m); S 2 ft (60 cm).

Michaelmas daisies (*Aster*) Lilac, pink, crimson, magenta, blue and white

Dividing and replanting border plants

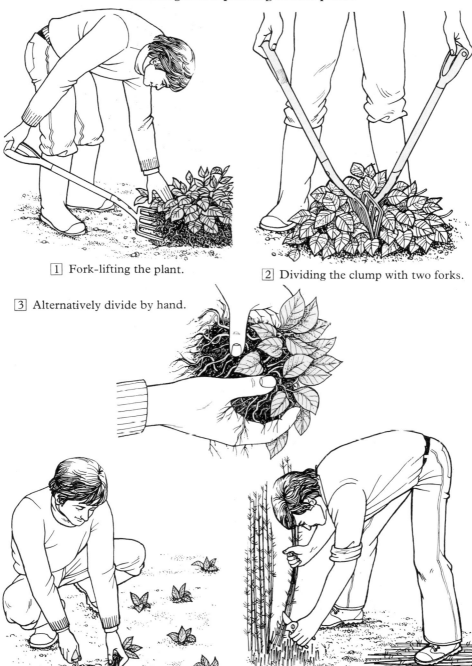

1 Fork-lifting the plant.

2 Dividing the clump with two forks.

3 Alternatively divide by hand.

4 Replanting the individual pieces.

5 Cutting down the dead stems in autumn.

in late summer/autumn. Prone to mildew (p. 82). Divide regularly. H 2–5 ft (60 cm–1.5 m); S 1½ ft (45 cm).

Phlox Sturdy and dramatic plants with white, pink, red or lilac flowers in late summer. Tough and reliable. H 2½–3½ ft (0.75–1.05 m); S 2 ft (60 cm).

Border plants for shade
Elephant's ears (*Bergenia*) Good in dry or moist soil. Large, rounded, evergreen leaves and red, pink or white flowers in spring. H 1–2 ft (30–60 cm); S 2 ft (60 cm).

Bugle (*Ajuga*) Creeping plants with blue flowers for moist soil. Many foliage colours including purple, bronze and variegated. H 6 in (15 cm); S 2 ft (60 cm).

Christmas rose (*Helleborus niger*) White flowers in winter, with weed smothering leaves later. Flowers prone to slug damage. H 1 ft (30 cm); S 15 in (38 cm).

Plaintain lily (*Hosta*) Best where soil is not too dry. Large leaves with a wide range of blue, yellow or white markings. Whitish flowers in summer and autumn. H 15–36 in (38–90 cm); S 2–3 ft (60–90 cm).

Lady's mantle (*Alchemilla*) Fresh green foliage followed by soft sprays of greeny yellow flowers in summer. Spreads by seeds, but not invasive. H 1½ ft (45 cm); S 2½ ft (75 cm).

Annuals, biennials and bedding
Annuals are plants which live for only one season. They are usually sown in the spring, flower in the summer and die in the autumn. Biennials are sown one year, flower the next and then die. Bedding plants are those, both annuals and biennials, which are planted out to provide a special seasonal display.

Annuals are amongst the easiest plants to grow, giving you a colourful display for very little outlay in terms of money or effort. Many of them are sown in the open garden where they are to flower (p. 12), thinned out and then pulled up and composted when they are finished. These varieties are known as 'hardy annuals' and make a very effective collective display.

☼ The soil is prepared for sowing

☼ Marking out the locations for several different hardy annual seed varieties.

1 Setting out bedding plants prior to planting.

2 After planting, water plants in well, incorporating some liquid feed.

(p. 12) and then the area which each variety is to occupy marked on the ground with a stick or with sand. Make each area at least 2 ft (60 cm) across and try not to make the shapes too regular. The taller varieties will look best at the back and the shorter ones at the front. Follow the instructions on the packet as to how far apart to sow them.

1 Bedding plants can best be treated in a similar way – set the plants out on the ground before planting them to make sure you get the best effect.

2 After planting water them in well

adding some liquid feed to the water to give them a good start. Many summer bedding plants are raised in a green-house because they need a long frost-free growing season to give their best (p. 60). Plant them out in late May or early June when danger of frost is past.

Biennials flower in spring and are usually sown in a seed bed outside in summer and transplanted (p. 14) to a wider spacing in mid-summer. Move them to their flowering situations in the autumn when all the summer plants are finished.

Easy hardy annuals

Alyssum Small, spreading plants with white, pink or purple flowers. Often sheds seed which comes up the following year. H 3–6 in (7.5–15 cm); S 6–9 in (15–23 cm).

Larkspur (*Delphinium*) Tall plants like delphiniums in pinks, blues and whites. Good cut flowers. H 1–4 ft (30 cm–1.2 m); S 1–2½ ft (30–75 cm).

Candytuft (*Iberis*) Small, dainty flower heads which bloom very soon after sowing. Colours are purples, lilacs, reds, pinks and white. H 9 in (23 cm); S 9 in (23 cm).

Marigold (*Calendula*) Easily grown with dandelion-like heads in orange and yellow. Good for cutting, but prone to mildew. H 1–2 ft (30–60 cm); S 1–1½ ft (30–45 cm).

Nasturtium (*Tropaeolum*) Climbing and bush types with red, orange or yellow flowers. Flowers best in hot dry sites. H 1 ft or 8 ft (0.3 or 2.4 m); S 1 ft or 3 ft (30 or 90 cm).

Sweet peas (*Lathyrus*) Sweetly scented climbers in a wide range of colours. Long flowering and good for cutting. H 6 ft (1.8 m); S 1 ft (30 cm).

Easy biennials

Wallflowers (*Cheiranthus*) Purple, reds, oranges, yellows and creamy shades. Very easy and tough, with a sweet scent in the evening and after rain. H 1–1½ ft (30–40 cm); S 9–12 in (23–30 cm).

Forget-me-nots (*Myosotis*) Bushy, rounded hummocks of blue. Tend to seed themselves for the following year. H 6–12 in (15–30 cm); S 6–12 in (15–30 cm).

Honesty (*Lunaria*) Flat silvery pods used for drying and preceded by purple flowers. Good in shade. H 3 ft (90 cm); S 1½ ft (45 cm).

Pansies (*Viola*) Brilliantly coloured flowers in all colours, blooming in mild spells in winter and in the spring. Use cheaper varieties for sowing outside. H 3–9 in (23–30 cm); S 6–9 in (23–30 cm).

Sweet William (*Dianthus*) Favourite cottage garden plants flowering in early summer. Flowers are red, pink and white. H 1–2 ft (30–60 cm); S 1–1¼ ft (30–38 cm).

Canterbury bell (*Campanula*) Tall, dramatic plants with large trumpets of blue, mauve, pink or white. H 1½–3 ft (45–90 cm); S 1–2 ft (30–60 cm).

Bulbs

There's no surer way to a colourful garden, especially in spring, than to plant bulbs; their appeal is universal. They can be planted in borders, in grass, in pots – anywhere that a splash of colour is needed. And bulbs are not just for spring – there are many summer flowering varieties too.

☼ In borders bulbs are best planted in groups – the impact is far greater than if they are scattered about or planted in rows. If you have an area of rough grass you can turn it into a feature by naturalizing daffodils, snowdrops, and winter aconites.

♣ Daffodils are best planted in random-shaped drifts over the area – just throw them out of the bag and plant them where they fall. A bulb planter is very handy for this or you can use a trowel.

Smaller bulbs are better in little clumps. 1 Remove the grass and set it on one side. 2 Dig a hole a couple of inches deep and set the bulbs in the hole – about half a dozen is an ideal number. Replace the soil and the grass. Scatter a handful of general fertilizer around each clump of bulbs when they are in flower. Don't forget that you must not cut the grass until about six weeks after the bulbs have flowered.

Lilies

Lilies need a little extra care compared with most bulbs. There are two types. Basal rooting types, such as *Lilium, candidum,* produce all their roots from the bottom of the bulb and are best planted in autumn with the nose of the bulb just below the surface. Stem rooting types, such as 'Enchantment', produce roots from the shoot as it grows up through the soil. These should be planted in spring, or in autumn if the soil is light, about 6 in (15 cm) deep. Lilies prefer a site in sun or partial shade with a soil enriched with organic matter such as peat.

Gladioli

Gladioli, too, need special treatment as they will not stand frost. The corms are planted 6 in (15 cm) deep in a sunny spot in spring so that the shoots appear after the last frost. In autumn, they are lifted and the corms dried off in the warm, then stored in a cool but frost-free place. All soil and loose skins should be removed. The baby corms can be retained and grown on for another 2–3 years before reaching flowering size.

Ground cover

Ground cover plants are those which spread outwards over the ground, smothering weeds with their foliage and making a carpet under shrubs and large border plants. Most are attractive in their own right and have this weed-smothering characteristic as a bonus. They give a more natural appearance to the garden and reduce weeding, provided they are given the chance to establish themselves.

☼ Planting bulbs in a group.

☘ Using a bulb planter for daffodil bulb.

1 Removing square of turf.

2 Setting out 7 small bulbs in the hole.

1 Positioning of young ground cover plants.

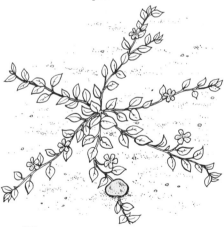

2 Weighting stem with stone to help rooting.

1 Preparation of the soil before planting is the same as for other plants. Ground coverers are best planted in informal groups around more substantial plants so that every corner is eventually filled with foliage.

2 Many achieve the smothering effect by means of stems which run over the surface of the soil – periwinkle for example. These can be encouraged by weighting down the shoots with stones to cover bare areas not yet colonized. A stone on a leaf joint is enough to get the stem to root.

You will find that many ground cover plants tend to collect leaves. These can be left amongst the foliage and stems; they will rot down bringing nourishment to the soil. Remember that early care and encouragement are vital if the plants are to do a good, weed-smothering job.

In the first instance you need only buy one of each plant. Most can then be easily increased the following year by layering or division and you will soon have plenty of plants.

Ground cover plants
Periwinkle (*Vinca*) Creeping stems with either green or variegated foliage plus blue or white flowers in spring. Plant 18 in (45 cm) apart.
Plantain lily (*Hosta*) Broad, spreading foliage so dense in summer that its absence in winter does not matter. Plant 18 in (45 cm) apart.
Cranesbill (*Geranium*) Not the pot plant, but an outdoor relation with pink or lilac flowers for many weeks and a determined tendency to spread without being rampant. Plant 15 in (38 cm) apart.
Lungwort (*Pulmonaria*) Greyish green leaves with white speckles and pink and blue flowers in spring. Spreads by seed as well as normal expansion. Plant 12 in (30 cm) apart.
Juniper (*Juniperus*) Prostrate types with green, yellowish or grey blue shoots on horizontal branches. Plant 4 ft (1.2 in) apart.

Fresh vegetables are one of the great delights that come as a reward for your efforts in the garden. Fortunately they are no more difficult to grow than other plants, and the effort required is not all that great. There are, though some important things to remember when starting on your first season of vegetable growing:

1 Choose a site that is as sunny as possible and certainly not overhung by trees.
2 Don't be too ambitious in the first year – it's better to grow a few crops well than to attempt a great many and fail with most of them.
3 Try not to grow the same vegetables in the same spot two years running. Pests and diseases may build up in the soil if you do.
4 Try to avoid using chemical sprays unless you have to.
5 Try the easy vegetables first – keep the more tricky types until you've grown the less demanding ones successfully.

The site should be prepared in the autumn and winter as described on p. 8 so that in the spring you are ready to make a start with sowings. Don't leave the preparation until spring or you will be behind all season. The crops I would suggest you try to start with are the salads – lettuces, radishes and spring onions, plus runner and French beans, onions, early potatoes (if you have space), cabbage, courgettes, and leeks.

Salads
Salads have the great advantage of giving you your reward quickly – in as little as a month with radishes.
☼ Lettuce is the basis of most salads and there are three types: (a) cos e.g. 'Lobjoits Green'; (b) cabbage e.g. 'All

☼ Types of lettuce (a) cos (b) cabbage (c) crisphead.

☼ Sowing radish seed.

♣ Salad onions.

the Year Round' and 'Buttercrunch' and (c) crisphead 'Webbs Wonderful' and 'Avoncrisp'.

Sow them in rows 1 ft (30 cm) apart and thin the seedlings first to 3 in (7.5 cm) and finally to 9 in (23 cm). Only sow a few feet at a time otherwise you will have a glut followed by a gap. Make these short row sowings every three weeks from early spring to mid-summer. Lettuces are vulnerable to slugs so use slug pellets among the plants. Plenty of water will be needed in summer and a little shade from taller crops will help to prevent bolting.

☼ Radishes need sowing every 10 days or so and, again, little and often is the key. You can usually find a home for them between rows of slower growing plants. Sow thinly and thin to $\frac{1}{2}$ in (13 mm) apart if necessary. Good varieties are 'French Breakfast' and 'Cherry Belle'.

♣ Salad onions are best sown thinly in a band about 3 in (7.5 cm) wide so that they don't need thinning out. Sow every two to three weeks from early spring to mid-summer. Grown this way and unthinned rather than in ordinary rows, they will stay at the harvesting stage for long enough to tide you through any unpredictable gaps.

Peas and beans

Beans have the great advantage of giving a large crop from relatively small areas while peas, although less productive, produce crops of superb flavour.

[1] Runner beans are probably the best bet.

[2] Sow them outside in the late spring, two seeds 3 in (8 cm) deep at the foot of each cane in a wigwam formation. If you particularly like runner beans two or three wigwams can be erected – any surplus beans are easy to

[1] Sowing runner beans seeds.

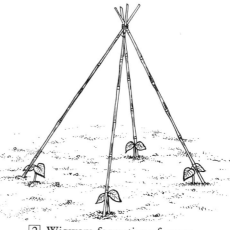

[2] Wigwam formation of canes.

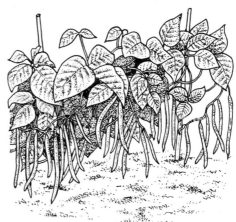

♣ French beans—sown in a single row.

freeze. Good varieties are 'Butler' and 'Achievement'.

♣ French beans are just as easy to grow, and particularly expensive in the shops. Sow them at the same time as runners. Sow one seed 2 in (5 cm) deep, every 6 in (15 cm) along the row and thin the plants to 1 ft (30 cm) apart when they come up. Fill any gaps by transplanting the thinnings. Sow again in the middle of summer. There are climbing versions of French beans which take up less space but generally speaking the flavour is less good. 'The Prince' is a good bush variety, and 'Largo' is a good climber.

Broad beans can be sown either in autumn or spring. For autumn sowings use the varieties 'The Sutton', a dwarf one, or 'Aquadulce Claudia' which is taller. For spring sowings, try 'The Sutton' or 'Imperial Green Longpod'.

✽ Sow in double rows 9 in (23 cm) apart with 3 ft (90 cm) between each pair, and set the seeds 3 in (7.5 cm) deep and 9 in (23 cm) apart. Put a few extras at the ends of the rows to fill gaps later. 'The Sutton' can go in single rows 2 ft (61 cm) apart. Taller varieties will need support as they grow.

Peas can be sown in autumn or

✽ Broad beans—sown in a double row.

spring depending on variety. In autumn try 'Feltham First' or 'Little Marvel', in spring 'Early Onward' and 'Hurst Green Shaft' are the most popular. Sow in 3 in (8 cm) deep and 9 in (23 cm) wide flat-bottomed drills made with a hoe and set the seeds 2–3 in (5–7.5 cm) apart. Netting is necessary for support and this should be set up as soon as the seed is in.

The peas will be much easier to pick and won't sprawl if well supported. Mice can be troublesome so set traps after sowing.

All these crops have a particular liking for rich soil which does not dry out. Take out a trench the depth of your spade and twice as wide where the peas and beans are to go, put some muck in the bottom and replace the soil a few weeks before sowing. Make sure the plants never dry out by watering regularly. Runner beans are especially susceptible to drought – the flowers fall off before the young beans form and you get no crop.

Root crops

The basic root crop is the **potato**. But potatoes take up a lot of space and in autumn and winter they can be bought cheaply by the sackload. Early potatoes are a different matter and well worth growing. They are more expensive to buy and you can improve on the flavour by growing your own. Varieties which are good for flavour and yield are 'Maris Bard' and 'Foremost'.

[1] Potatoes are grown from seed potatoes, which are small, specially selected spuds, that should be free of disease. Seed potatoes are bought in early spring and must be set out in the light to start to grow before being planted. Put one tuber in each section of an egg box and stand the boxes in a place where they will get plenty of light and which is frost free though not hot – a garage window, the windowsill of a spare room or a frost-free greenhouse are ideal.

Planting time is in early spring.

[2] Dig a trench the depth and width of the spade and take the soil to the other end of the potato plot.

[3] Line the trench with an inch or two of organic matter – the first grass cuttings are ideal – and then put an inch of soil on top.

[4] Set the seed potatoes with the shoots uppermost 12 in (30 cm) apart. Dig the next trench 2 ft (30 cm) away and use the soil to fill the first trench. Carry on until the last trench and fill this one with the soil from the first.

When the shoots first come through there will be a danger of frost damage, so, if frost is forecast, cover the shoots with newspaper held down with stones. You should be able to dig the first roots by mid-summer. Dig from the side of the row to avoid damaging the tubers.

Beetroot probably suffers from fewer pests and diseases than any other vegetable and so is not difficult to grow well. One slight problem is that most beetroot seed comes in clusters – three or four seeds are grouped together in one capsule. The result is that if they all come up you have a number of plants growing at the same spot. These must be thinned to one plant. Sow from late spring to early summer in rows 15 in (38 cm) apart and thin to $4\frac{1}{2}$ in (11 cm) and then 9 in (23 cm).

The only other difficulty can be drought. If a deluge comes after a long dry spell the roots may be split making them unusable. Good varieties are 'Boltardy' and 'Cheltenham Green Top'.

1 Seed potatoes in egg boxes.

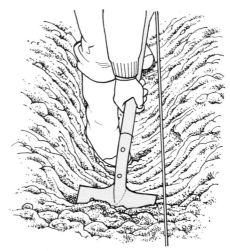

2 Digging a potato trench.

3 Fork in organic matter/compost.

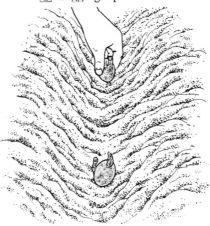

4 Planting the seed potatoes.

Carrots are more difficult to grow, mainly because they often succumb to a very nasty pest – carrot fly (p. 84).

Sow the seeds of salad carrots – good varieties are 'Nantes Express' and 'Kundulus' – from spring to mid-summer in rows 6 in (15 cm) apart and carrots for the winter in summer in rows 12 in (30 cm) apart. Varieties for storing include 'Chantenay Red Cored' and 'Autumn King'. In both cases try and sow thinly. Salad carrots need not be thinned; maincrop ones should be thinned to 4 in (10 cm) and the thinnings removed. Use a soil insecticide in the seed drills to avoid carrot fly.

☼ **Parsnips** are easier but need a long growing season. Sow in early spring putting three seeds every 9 in (23 cm) in rows 12 in (30 cm) apart (p. 44). Sow a few radishes in the gap. Parsnips are very slow to come up so the radishes

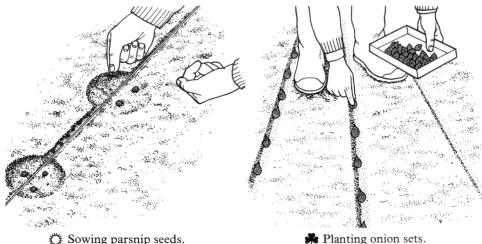

☼ Sowing parsnip seeds.   ♣ Planting onion sets.

will help show you where the rows are. When the parsnips germinate remove the two weakest ones at each point leaving the best to grow on.

♣ **Onions** are easy to grow from sets. Sets are tiny onion bulbs which quickly grow to full size after planting in early spring. Set them 6 in (15 cm) apart in rows 6 in (15 cm) apart so that the tips just peep through the soil. If the birds pull them out, re-plant them. Keep them well watered and weeded and they will be ready in late summer. Onion sets for autumn planting are now widely available and can be harvested several weeks earlier than those planted in spring.

Brassicas

This is the general name given to all members of the cabbage family and includes cabbages, cauliflowers, sprouts, broccoli, and kale. They are all easily transplanted so are grown in seed beds and planted out when they are about 4–6 in (10–15 cm) high (p. 14). All of them prefer a limy soil and so a dressing of lime on the seed bed and before planting out is very helpful (un-less your soil is chalky). All brassicas suffer from two dreaded diseases – clubroot and cabbage root fly (p. 84).

The simplest of all to grow are cabbages and starting with these will give encouraging results quickly. Kale and broccoli are fairly easy, sprouts have a few problems while cauliflowers are often quite difficult to grow well, so progress to these steadily.

Cabbages are sown in a seed bed in spring to provide crops in summer, autumn and winter, and in summer for crops the following spring. Sow the seeds thinly in short rows spaced 9 in (23 cm) apart. There are plenty of varieties to choose from – round headed and pointed, red and green. For summer and autumn harvesting try 'Hispi' and 'Minicole'; for winter, 'January King', and for spring, 'April'. 'Red Drumhead' is a good red cabbage. When planting, space the plants out 14 in (35 cm) apart in rows the same distance apart. This will give you the highest yield of good sized, though not enormous, heads. Plant with a trowel leaving a slight depression around each plant then give a good drink from the watering can to minimize wilting and to make sure the plant takes root quickly.

Other crops

Like cabbages, **leeks** need a seed bed. Sow them in spring and when they are about 9 in (23 cm) high lift them and plant them out 9 in (23 cm) apart each way.

[1] Before planting trim the tops and the roots by a third.

[2] Make holes with a rake handle or dibber, drop the young plants in and water them in well [3]. They will eventually produce a long white stem. Good varieties are 'Musselburgh' and 'The Lyon'.

Marrows and courgettes can be raised indoors or outside. Outdoors, sow pairs of seeds 2½ ft (75 cm) apart in late spring and put a jam jar, preferably a 2 lb one, over each sown spot. At the beginning of summer remove the jar and the weaker of the seedlings.

The seeds can also be sown indoors (usually with better results), also in late spring. Set one seed in each 3 in (7.5 cm) pot of seed compost, water them in and put them in the airing cupboard. As soon as a shoot appears move each pot to a warm windowsill and your plants will be ready to plant out in early summer. It is important to keep them well watered, and feed them every ten days with a liquid feed. Courgettes are only baby marrows and are cut when 4–6 in (10–15 cm) long. If you leave them they will grow into marrows but the supply of courgettes will dry up. A good variety of marrow is 'Long Green Bush' and the best courgette is 'Zucchini'.

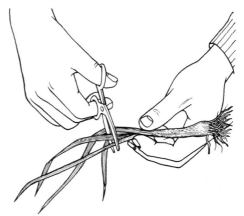

[1] Trimming young leek plant.

[2] Making planting holes for leeks.

[3] Watering the planted leeks.

[1] Planting young strawberry plant.

[2] Inserting mat to keep fruit off soil.

[3] Netting strawberry plants.

Strawberries

Although many people think of fruit growing as a risky and often unproductive enterprise there is nothing to compare with succulent juicy fruit that's grown at home. Strawberries are a firm favourite and fortunately they are not difficult to grow. With modern varieties the problem of the glut when they are cheap in the shops can be overcome and you can usually beat shop-bought fruit for flavour.

[1] It's best to start with pot grown plants; these can be planted in late summer and autumn, and will produce fruit the following year. You can also buy plants in bundles with bare roots but these take longer to establish. Prepare well by digging and enriching the soil (p. 8) and plant out the young plants 18 in (45 cm) apart with the rows 2 ft (60 cm) apart. Make sure the plants are well watered. A site in full sun or one shaded for part, but not all of the day is ideal.

In the spring when the plants come into flower keep the beds free of weeds and cut off any runners that creep across the ground from the plants. Look out for greenfly and spray if necessary.

[2] When the fruits start to swell, put something under the plants to keep the fruits off the soil. Special mats are available or you can use straw, black polythene or squares of carpet underlay.

[3] It's also a good idea to net the plants to prevent birds getting the fruit. After picking, cut off all the old leaves and keep taking off the runners for the rest of the year. Strawberries need replacing after four years as they tend to get an incurable virus disease which reduces the crop. Try and plant in a new spot.

Good varieties to give you a crop over a long period are 'Tantallon', 'Saladin', 'Troubadour' and 'Aromel'. If you only have a space for a few plants, choose 'Aromel'.

Raspberries

Raspberry plants, known as 'canes', are planted in the autumn or winter, after the leaves have fallen. They need support as they grow, so erect a stout post at the end of each row and run wires between then at 2, 3½ and 5 ft (60, 96 and 150 cm) above ground. 1 Set the plants out 18 in (45 cm) apart and cut the canes, which will usually consist of one long stem, down to 9 in (23 cm) 2 . They will not fruit in their first season but will establish well. Tie in and space out the shoots as they grow and keep the weeds down. 3 After they fruit the following summer, cut out at the base all those shoots which have carried fruit and leave the new ones. Tie them in as they grow.

Birds can often be a problem so ideally the row should be netted to protect the young fruits. To keep weeds down between the rows, a weed preventer (which kills weeds as they germinate) is a good idea once the rows are established, and make sure you give extra water if there is a dry spell after flowering.

Raspberry canes can produce good crops for up to 10 years but shoots which start appearing away from the row should be removed, together with any weak ones, to leave the canes spaced about 9 in (23 cm) apart. Good varieties are 'Malling Delight' and 'Leo'. There are also autumn-fruiting varieties such as 'September' and 'Zeva'. These are grown in a similar way but are pruned in late winter.

1 Planting raspberry canes.

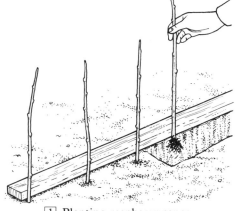

2 Cut back canes to 9 in (23 cm).

3 Summer pruning on established canes.

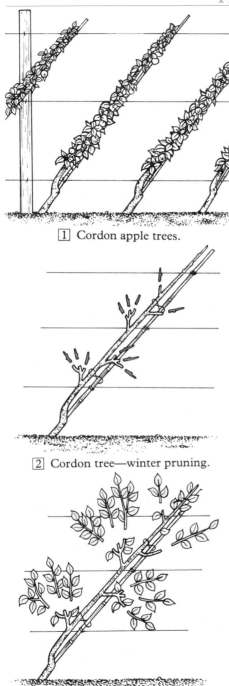

1 Cordon apple trees.

2 Cordon tree—winter pruning.

3 Cordon tree—summer pruning.

All the stems are cut down hard to the ground and the new shoots which grow carry fruit in the autumn, so extending the season. To keep your plants in good health feed them with sulphate of potash after picking – a handful to each yard of row.

Apples and pears

Many people find an old apple or pear tree in the garden when they take over a house and wonder how to cope with it. In many cases it will be too big to do anything with but it is helpful to thin it out and remove from the centre any crowded and crossing branches which form a tangled mass. Smaller trees can be pruned more carefully by removing all but 2 in (5 cm) of the new side shoots and removing the occasional larger branch to give an even spacing. Feeding is helpful, especially if trees are grown in grass. Put on growmore at the rate of 4 oz/sq yd (135g/sq m) under the tree in early spring.

1 If you're planting new apples it is a good idea to plant small trees, especially cordons. These are small, manageable trees which never grow bigger than 6 ft (1.8 m) so are easy to look after. They consist basically, of a single stem on which the fruit is carried. They are planted 2½ ft (75 cm) apart at an angle of about 45° and tied to a framework of wires similar to that used for raspberries. Again a dose of fertilizer every spring is helpful.

2 Prune them in winter by shortening all side shoots to 2 in (5 cm) and again in mid-summer by shortening new shoots by a similar amount 3 .

Don't shorten the tip until it has reached the top wire. You usually need two varieties which flower at the same time near to each other to get good crops, 'James Grieve' and 'Worcester

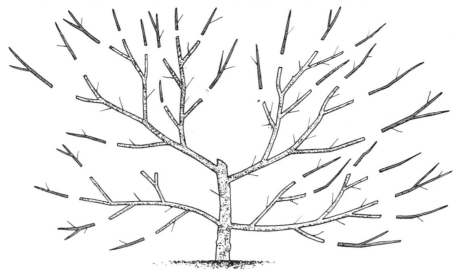

☼ Gooseberry—winter pruning.

Pearmain' for example. 'Discovery' is an exception as it will produce fruit on its own.

For pears try 'Conference' and 'Williams'.

Blackcurrants and gooseberries
These are robust bushes which present no great difficulties apart from the attentions of birds and the occasional special problem.

Currants These take up a fair amount of room but fortunately very little time so if you have the space, grow them. Plant the bushes 5 ft (1.5 m) apart between autumn and spring but make sure you prepare the soil really well first (p. 8) – the more muck the better. Cut the plants down to about 2 in (5 cm) when you plant them. They will produce no fruit at all in the first year but after that they should fruit regularly. Keep the plants weed free and feed them early every spring with 4 oz of growmore per square yard.

Pruning can be made less complicated than you'd think. When harvesting, simply cut out each branch that has fruit on it. You can then pick the berries in comfort and the job of pruning is done too – it couldn't be simpler.

Apart from birds, and netting will take care of them, the main problem is virus disease. This is carried by a tiny mite which makes the buds swell up to twice their normal size. Pick off swollen buds in late winter. If there are a lot, burn the bush as it will never crop well. Good varieties are 'Ben More', 'Ben Lomond' and 'Malling Jet'.

Gooseberries. These are grown on a short 'leg' to help keep the fruit off the ground. After planting prune back all shoots by about half. Feed every spring as for blackcurrants and keep them weed free.

☼ As to pruning, the aim should be to create a bowl-shaped plant with no branches in the centre so that you don't scratch your hands when picking the fruit. For the first three years cut back all shoots by half in winter and then switch to summer pruning, cutting back all side shoots to about five leaves, including the tip branches when they are long enough.

The main problem is mildew. Spray with a fungicide at the first sign and again two weeks later. Good varieties are 'Jubilee' and 'Careless'. Red and white currants are grown like gooseberries, rather than like blackcurrants.

6
GREENHOUSE GROWING

Greenhouses

Even in today's era of ever-rising prices, a basic aluminium greenhouse represents superb value for money. You can grow vast quantities of tomatoes, out-of-season lettuce and other salads, plus pot plants and bedding plants, all without any heat.

☼ The basic greenhouse can only be rudimentary and you will need one or two extras to get the best from it. You will find that aluminium-framed greenhouses are cheaper than timber ones, the latter being more elegant but needing more maintenance. If you buy a more expensive greenhouse (and especially if it is larger than the basic 8 × 6 ft (2.4 × 1.8 m)) one, you may well find that the company has a scheme whereby they erect it for you. This is well worth taking up as erecting a large greenhouse is quite an undertaking. You can avoid all the anguish by getting the experts to do it for you.

✿ These days conservatories are becoming much more popular. Not only are they more attractive than they once were, they are also more reasonable in price. Don't forget that they add to the value of your house too, being an ideal sun room as well as a place to grow plants. Electricity and water are to hand and you can have these useful services installed cheaply. What is more, if you want to heat your conservatory you can run an extra radiator off the central heating system.

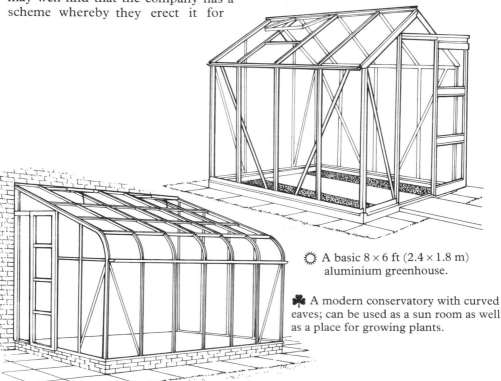

☼ A basic 8 × 6 ft (2.4 × 1.8 m) aluminium greenhouse.

✿ A modern conservatory with curved eaves; can be used as a sun room as well as a place for growing plants.

Greenhouse equipment

Although you can get by with very few extras to make the most of your greenhouse one or two accessories will be a great help.

Extra ventilators In summer a small greenhouse can get very hot very quickly if there is insufficient ventilation. In an 8 × 6 ft (2.4 × 1.8 m) greenhouse you should have at least two ventilators in opposite sides of the roof plus one louvre type ventilator at the bottom of each side. This will give a good air flow.

Automatic openers Invaluable if you are at work all day as the weather can change very quickly. They are available for standard and louvre type ventilators and will open and close the ventilators at presct temperatures.

Staging Very useful for just one side so that pots are brought up to a height at which they can be managed easily. Self-assembly aluminium staging is ideal.

Heater Not vital, but if you can keep your greenhouse frost free you can carry plants like geraniums and fuchsias through the winter and raise tender bedding plants. The cheapest to run is

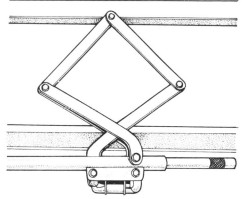

Automatic ventilator opener.

Electric greenhouse heater.

probably an extra radiator off the central heating system, followed by a mains gas-fired heater, a bottled gas heater and paraffin heater. Electric heaters, though, are the best bet. They provide clean, dry heat (especially important in winter) and can be connected to a thermostat for maximum economy. With gas and paraffin prices rising more rapidly, electricity is becoming a relatively less expensive proposition.

Automatic watering Simple automatic systems help you look after

Automatic watering for pot plants and seed trays.

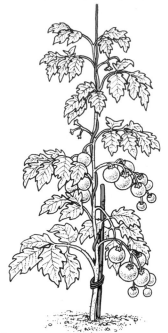

☼ Cane and string support for tomato plant.

♣ Supporting tomato plant in growing bag.

your plants in the summer months without constant recourse to the watering can. One type has a tiny pipe running into each pot and in another the pipe feeds a water holding mat which covers the staging and from which the pots draw water. This can be connected to a mains water supply or a water reservoir in the greenhouse.

Tomatoes

☼ The one crop everyone likes to grow in the greenhouse and fortunately it is not difficult to raise good supplies. The simplest plan for an unheated greenhouse is to buy young plants in late spring. These can then be either planted in the soil in the greenhouse or in growing bags. You will find that you can only grow tomatoes in the same piece of soil for a few years without disease building up and the crop being ruined. After four years, in alternate borders of the greenhouse, change to growing bags.

The soil is best prepared with plenty of peat or garden compost before planting. Set the plants 18 in (45 cm) apart and support them by knocking in a short cane alongside each plant and tying some polypropylene string to the cane. Fix the other end tightly to a strut in the roof. You can buy special fixing clips for aluminium struts. The tomato stem can then be twisted round the twine as it grows.

♣ In growing bags put three plants in each bag, loop the twine under the bag by each plant and tie it before running it up to the roof.

Water all plants well and feed with a special tomato feed every week once tiny tomatoes are seen on the plants.

Remove any side shoots when they are small. Make sure you check the watering every day in summer, plants in growing bags need especially large amounts.

Whitefly is the most common pest and a greenhouse fumigant is the best treatment.

Varieties to look out for are 'Alicante', 'Shirley' and 'Sweet 100'.

Peppers

These are just as easy to grow as tomatoes but small enough to be grown in pots on the staging if necessary. Unfortunately the plants are less easy to buy, but they can be raised on a warm windowsill by sowing seeds in early spring. Transfer the seedlings to 3 in (7.5 cm) pots of peat-based potting compost and plant three plants in a growing bag or one in a 9 in (23 cm) pot. Whitefly is often a problem with peppers too.

♧ Removing first 'baby' pepper fruit.

♧ Although it will delay ripening of the first fruit, it is wise to remove the first baby pepper when it is still small; leaving it will prevent the growth of other fruits. Feed the plants once a week. Good varieties are 'Canape' and 'Early Prolific'.

❀ **Aubergines** are grown in the same way but are more susceptible to pests.

Cucumbers

Although these require rather different conditions from tomatoes they can be grown together in the same greenhouse, but you will not get the best out of either. Again you can buy plants in late spring or raise them yourself from seed.

Put two seeds in each 3 in (7.5 cm) pot and gently pull out the weaker one if both come up. The seeds need a high temperature so it is best to put them in the airing cupboard until you see the first signs of sprouting, then transfer

❀ Aubergine plant with fruits.

them to a windowsill. Alternatively plant two to a growing bag or plant direct in the soil.

For support tie some pea and bean netting to the bag with polypropylene twine and run it up the roof, securing it well. As the plants grow train them up the net. Pinch out side shoots two leaves after a female flower (one with a

◊ Cucumber—female flower.

tiny cucumber behind it ◊) and pinch out the tip when it gets to the top. Feed once a week with tomato food and keep well watered. Remove any male flowers (those which lack miniature cucumbers behind the petals) before they open. Pollinated female flowers produce bitter fruits. Varieties sold as 'all female' produce very few male flowers, but it's still worth keeping your eye open for them.

Good varieties to look out for are 'Telegraph Improved' and 'Fembaby'.

Flowers

The easiest plants to grow in a cold greenhouse are **bulbs**. All spring bulbs can be forced like hyacinths (p. 58). Small bulbs like crocuses are especially successful when grown in the greenhouse from planting to budding.

⃝1 Set the bulbs, keeping one colour to each pot, half way down a half pot or bowl in a peat-based compost. Plant in the autumn and keep the greenhouse cold, with the ventilators always open until the frosts start. Then keep them closed only when it is frosty or there are cold winds. Other bulbs that can be housed in a cold house until flowering are daffodils, hyacinths, iris and grape hyacinth. ⃝2 When they bloom, bring them indoors.

Pot plants can also be grown in unheated conditions. Dwarf hardy annuals make good pot plants especially pot marigold (*Calendula*). The variety 'Fiesta Gitana' is especially suitable. Sow at any time from February to September – those sown after mid-August will probably not flower until the following year. Transfer them to $4\frac{1}{2}$ in (11.5 cm) pots and they will make delightful little plants.

In summer French marigolds can be sown for pot plants in autumn. Stocks make good dramatic plants with a lovely scent and the little *Phlox drummondii* with its starry flowers is excellent, too.

☼ For flowering in the spring polyanthuses are superb, and the primroses too. These can be grown in 3 in pots. Pansies will flower right through the winter if sown in early summer.

Rock plants, especially the smaller kinds, do very well in pots. They can be stood outside in the summer and early autumn and brought in when the tomatoes come out. They will flower before rock plants outside and start the year with a delightful sparkle of colour. Gentians, rock pinks, pasque flower, houseleeks, stonecrops, edelweiss, alpine primroses and violas are all worth trying. With the crocus and irises already mentioned you will achieve a fine spring show. There are two requirements to bear in mind with these plants: firstly they must have a free-draining compost and secondly they must not get too hot. This is one of the reasons why extra ventilation in a greenhouse is so important. If the plants get overheated, not only will the compost get too dry but more importantly the plants will get far too leggy and lank.

1 Planting bulbs in peat-based compost.

2 Miniature iris (*left*) and crocus (*right*) bulbs in flower.

☼ Potting polyanthus in a 3 in (7.5 cm) pot.

Foliage house plants

In recent years the growing of house plants has really taken off. Although we haven't yet caught up with the continentals, especially the Dutch, we're well on the way.

Foliage house plants (those that are grown more for their leaves than their often insignificant flowers) are generally the easiest. There are types for all situations in the house and, provided they are given the conditions they require, you should have few problems.

More mistakes are made over the watering of house plants than over any other aspect of cultivation. The amount of water a plant needs depends on a number of things such as the time of year, size of plant in relation to its pot, and its position in the house. Most plants need more water in the summer than in winter. If a plant is in a pot that is too small it will also need more water. Plants on sunny windowsills in warm rooms will need more than plants in cooler and shadier areas. The only answer is to test each plant regularly by sticking your finger in the soil in the pot. If it seems dry, water it.

Easy plants

☼ **Ivy (*Hedera*)** Happy in cool rooms but if overwatered the bottom leaves go yellow and drop off. Train it on a wire or cane. Best in bright light but out of direct sun.

Wandering Jew (*Tradescantia*) A very easy and strong growing trailer which puts up with almost anything. Cuttings root easily in jam jars of water.

Rubber plant (*Ficus*) Happy in light or shade but cold draughts and over watering in winter are fatal.

Spider Plant (*Chlorophytum*) Almost indestructible! Generous feeding and watering in summer and almost no watering in winter suits it best. Easily increased from the young plantlets carried on arching stems.

Plants needing extra care

Maidenhair fern Best in a light spot but not bright sun and also grows well in shade. Needs a moist atmosphere so stand the pot on a dish of wet gravel.

❀ **Iron cross begonia (*Begonia masoniana*)** Bright position but out of full sunlight is best. Keep water off the leaves or they may rot.

♧ **Dumb cane (*Dieffenbachia*)** Best fairly warm, 60°F (15°C) or more, and a spray over every day helps. Keep out of draughts.

Zebra plant (*Aphelandra*) Must be kept moist, but not sodden, at all times. Produces yellow flowers if not fed too much.

Angel's wings (*Caladium*) Dies down in the winter. Water well while growing and keep in a light spot. Keep on the dry side (but not dust dry) when it dies down.

Many foliage plants like a moist atmosphere and this can be created by standing the plant in a large saucer part filled with gravel which is kept moist, or by putting the pot in a larger one and the space between the two filled with peat which is kept moist.

Flowering pot plants

Many flowering pot plants are looked upon as an extra-long-lasting bunch of flowers! Hanging on to poinsettias and chrysanthemums bought as pot plants is not really worthwhile. Others, like geraniums and African violets, are worth keeping and are not difficult to grow. The easiest to grow yourself are probably bulbs. Hyacinths, for example can be forced for Christmas if you follow the right procedure. Firstly

☼ Ivy—best trained on wire, as here, or on canes.

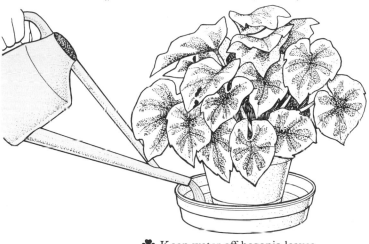

☘ Keep water off begonia leaves.

♣ Dumb cane (*Dieffenbachia*) appreciates a daily water spray.

1 Planting prepared hyacinth bulbs.

2 Covering potted bulbs with moist peat.

3 Bring indoors when shoots are 2 in (5 cm) long.

always buy 'prepared' bulbs, these are the only ones which will flower at Christmas.

1 Plant them with $\frac{1}{2}$ in (13 mm) between bulbs in a pot of bulb fibre with the tips peeping through the compost. Put them in a cold, dark place.

2 The simplest choice is probably at the base of a north wall where they should be covered with moist peat or sand.

3 When the shoots are 2 in (5 cm) long they should be brought into a cool room and then into a warmer room as they come into flower.

Flowering plants are, in general, a little more sensitive than foliage plants.

☼ **African violets (*Saintpaulia*)** Likes a bright, but not sunlit, windowsill (possibly facing north). Don't overwater but keep a moist atmosphere by standing the plant in a saucer of damp gravel. Remove dead flowers to prevent rot.

Christmas cactus (*Schlumbergera*) Likes some sun and can be stood outside in summer. Do not move the plant after the buds have formed or they may well drop off.

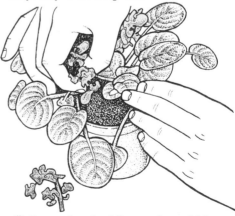

☼ Removing dead flowers from African violet.

Cyclamen A cool windowsill in good light is best, excessive central heating fatal. Stop watering in late spring and keep dry until late summer when the fat tubers are re-potted and started into growth again.

Chrysanthemum Keep in good light, at not more than 65°F (18°C), and moist but not sodden. Plant them in the garden after flowering (where they will grow very tall and flower very late).

Poinsettias Keep the temperature above 60°F (15°C) and feed once a week. Water when the compost feels dry. Can be kept cut down for another year as a green foliage plant.

Amaryllis (*Hippeastrum*) Dramatic flowers from large bulbs sold in autumn. Easy to flower once. To flower again feed well after flowering. When the foliage starts to yellow cut it off an inch above the bulb and keep somewhere warm and dry until a new shoot starts to appear, then water.

Watering is a difficult business. Pots should have a gap of $\frac{1}{4}$ $\frac{1}{2}$ in (6–13 mm) between the compost and the rim of the pot. This space should be filled with water from a narrow spouted can and left to drain through. The space should be filled again until water runs from the base of the pot. After 15 minutes, tip away any water remaining in the saucer. Never leave pots standing in water. Some plants, like cyclamen, do not like water splashing on the crown of the plant. These plants can have water put in the saucer until no more is soaked up and the surplus is then thrown away.

Compost

You can now buy special house plant potting compost which is very good for all house plants. It is similar to the compost used by the pot-plant growers so when you repot there will be no incompatibility problems. Composts known as the John Innes type used to be used widely but are now less common. These contain high-quality, sterilized garden soil as well as the peat, sand and nutrients found in modern composts. These are very good, though variable in quality, but not compatible with the compost most house-plant nurserymen use.

Feeding

The simplest way to feed is to use a liquid fertilizer. This is used about once a week during the growing season, but check the directions on the pack.

✿ To avoid the possibility of forgetting to feed, fertilizer spikes are now available, these are pushed into the soil and provide plant food for up to two months. Specialist house-plant fertilizers are also now available including types for African violets and other flowering house plants, and others for green foliage plants and variegated foliage plants.

✿ Inserting a fertilizer spike.

[1] Firming the compost in the corners of the tray.

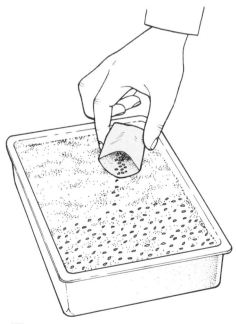

[2] Sowing seeds evenly over the surface.

Making more plants

There are two basic methods of making plants – by sowing seeds and taking cuttings. Annuals, bedding plants and border plants are grown from seed while shrubs and most house plants are grown from cuttings.

Seed Sowing

Sowing seed takes a little care. Look in the packet first and see how much seed you've got. In most cases a half tray [$8\frac{1}{2} \times 6\frac{1}{2}$ in (215×165 mm)] is quite big enough, or for very small numbers a 4 in (10 cm) pot is sufficient. It must be clean to prevent disease infection.

Compost is crucial. Garden soil is useless as it contains weed seeds as well as fungi and bacteria that will attack delicate young seedlings. It's badly drained when used in containers, too. Buy some special seed sowing compost from the garden centre or use one of the multi-purpose types.

[1] Make sure the compost is moist, then fill the seed tray lightly to the top and then firm it with the bottom of another tray and make sure that the corners are firm. This will leave a gap of $\frac{1}{4}$–$\frac{1}{2}$ in (6–13 mm).

[2] Sow the seeds evenly over the surface. Large seeds can be spaced out individually, smaller ones sprinkled as evenly as possible: $\frac{1}{8}$–$\frac{1}{4}$ in (3–6 mm) apart is about right for small seeds. Dahlias, sweet peas and the like can be spaced out an inch (2.5 cm) apart.

[3] Now, using a wire kitchen sieve, cover the seeds with a layer of compost. It should be as thick as the seeds themselves. For small seeds this means no more than two shakes and for tiny seeds don't bother. To make sure the compost is moist, stand the pot in a washing up bowl for ten minutes then take it out and let it drain. Cover the top with

clingfilm and put it in a warm spot such as near the central heating boiler, near a radiator or in the airing cupboard. If it is in the light cover with newspaper as well.

Check each day to see if there are signs of growth and as soon as tiny shoots appear, take off the paper, or remove the pots from the airing cupboard, and stand them in good light. When the seedlings are recognizable as tiny plants remove the clingfilm.

Apart from those you have space sown, the plants will soon need to be transferred to a new tray ('pricked out'). Fill a seed tray in the same way as for seed sowing. Then using a pencil or small dibber, ease out each seedling in turn from the seed tray or pot, keeping as much soil on the fine roots as possible and holding each seedling by one of its leaves. Make a hole with the pencil in the new compost, slide the seedling into the hole and nestle a little compost round the roots. In a half tray you will get 20 seedlings – five one way, four the other. Again soak them in the washing up bowl and then stand them on a tray. Where they go from this stage depends very much on the plant in question and most seed packets will give you a good idea. Most seedlings need some protection from the elements by being placed in a greenhouse or frame until they are established.

Large seeds that quickly make strong plants like sweet peas, runner beans, cucumbers and marrows can be sown in small pots. If you have plenty of space sow one seed in each pot and discard any pots where nothing appears. Otherwise sow two and pull up the weaker seedling if both germinate. A word of warning: the compost that remains after pricking out should not be used again for seed sowing. It can be

3 Covering the seeds with a layer of compost.

☼ Seed-raising kit: pre-sown seeds germinating.

used for re-potting or for filling containers outside.

☼ Seed-raising kits are now available which make the whole business easier. These have the seeds pre-sown for you in special compost and all you do is water them and keep them warm.

☼ Inserting cuttings in jam-jar of water to induce rooting.

Plants from cuttings

Some plants are so easy to root from cuttings that you wonder why they cost so much in the shops. For simple plants like busy Lizzies, African violets and tradescantia the method is easy.

Fill a jam jar almost to the brim with water. Cut a piece of kitchen foil an inch bigger than the jam jar all round, put it over the top and fold down the sides. Using the sharp point of a kitchen knife make some very small holes in the foil through which to push the cuttings.

Cut off 3 in (7.5 cm) tips of wandering Jew and busy lizzie shoots with a sharp pair of scissors or a razor blade. Trim off the leaves on the bottom half of the cutting and then re-cut the base just underneath a leaf joint. African violets should have single leaves cut off with as much stalk as possible.

☼ The cuttings are then pushed through the holes in the foil and put on a windowsill. Roots are often visible in a matter of days and when they are about an inch long the plants can be put in pots of compost.

Partly fill a 3 in (7.5 cm) flower pot with potting compost and press it down gently. Sit the rooted cutting on the top of the compost. If the lowest leaf is more than $\frac{1}{2}$ in (13 mm) below the rim of the pot add a little extra compost, if it's less remove a little.

Then add more compost jiggling the cutting slightly so that compost filters amongst the roots and carry on until the compost is level with a rim of the pot. Press gently with the fingers and level off leaving a $\frac{1}{4}$ in (6 mm) space at the top of the pot. Water gently with a can fitted with a fine sprinkler head or 'rose'.

✿ Cuttings, inserted in a tray of compost, are then covered with cling film to prevent loss of moisture.

Many cuttings, although easy to root, cannot be rooted in water. These include fuchsias, geraniums, ivy and many deciduous shrubs. Cuttings are taken in the same way as buzy lizzies – the best time is during the summer. Instead of rooting them in water they must go in pots or trays of compost which are made up in the same way as those for seed sowing.

Rooting powder is a useful aid to rooting these types. After the cutting is prepared, the base is dipped lightly in the powder which sticks to the cutting and this helps it root more quickly. Make a hole in the compost with a dibber or pencil, put the cutting in up to its lower leaves and gently press the compost around it. Water it in gently and this will help settle the soil round the stems.

If you're using a pot put it in a polythene bag and sit it somewhere warm and light, but not in bright sun-

light. If the cuttings have slightly hairy foliage, like geraniums, put in a hoop to keep the polythene off the leaves.

✿ A seed tray can be put inside a white carrier bag or the whole tray, cuttings and all, covered in clingfilm. The air space under the polythene can heat up a lot in sunshine so keep the sun off by shading with paper if necessary. You will know when the cuttings have rooted because they will start to grow, so resist the temptation to dig them up every few days to see how they're getting on.

Plants like geraniums which root fairly easily and grow quickly once rooted, can also be rooted in individual pots. Use a 3 in (7.5 cm) pot and fill with a peat-based potting compost. Cuttings are taken in the same way although geraniums will often root uncovered out of bright sunshine.

8
LAWNS

Making a lawn

It is not often that you see a really good lawn. Even lawns that impress at some times of the year are often full of moss and look much worse after a drought. The answer is to start off well. It can be arduous to prepare properly, but it must be done. Spring and autumn are the best times.

Ideally the ground should be dug, but if you lack the time or the inclination to do this then you can rotavate the whole area; this is much easier than digging. All weeds should be killed off with a weed killer first. If you can get hold of large quantities of organic matter – a bulk load of peat, for instance, or mushroom compost – spread it on the surface and rotavate it in.

[1] [2] Tread the area well and rake level roughly.

You can make your lawn from turf or seed. Turf is more expensive but can be walked on after six weeks. Seed is cheaper, though it will be some months before it will be able to take normal traffic, but you can choose the type of grass you want. Whether you choose turf or seed, rake in 2 oz (60 g) of growmore per square yard (metre) before starting.

[3] Turf comes in pieces which are usually 3 × 1 ft (90 × 30 cm) and you should first lay a strip all round the edge. Then, starting on the straightest side, lay a plank on the edge and working from it put down the next row.

[4] Make sure the joints do not align – bond the turves like brickwork.

[5] When you've finished rake in some old potting compost, sharp sand or sifted soil to fill any cracks then water well.

If you sow seed the first thing to do is buy the right type. It comes in hard-

[1] Ground preparation—treading the area.

[2] Ground preparation—raking thoroughly.

wearing mixtures, mixtures for shady areas and mixtures for a bowling-green finish.

[6] Grass seed is usually sown at the rate of about $1\frac{1}{2}$ oz/yd² (50 g/m²). Weigh out the amount recommended on the packet, put it in an old yoghurt pot and mark the level with a felt tipped pen.

Lawn from turf

3 Laying the first turves.

4 Bond the turves like brickwork.

5 Raking in compost/sand to fill
any cracks.

Now, using two garden lines, lay out a
strip one yard wide.

7 Garden canes are then laid across
at 3 ft intervals giving a sequence of
square yards.

8 One fill of the pot to the marked
level goes on each square yard.

Lawn from seed

6 Using a yoghurt pot to make a
standard seed measure.

7 Marking out square yard areas.

8 Sowing the grass seed.

Move the string and canes until you have finished the plot. Now rake the area well – though you won't be able to cover all the seed. Do not roll it. Most seed is treated to be unpalatable, though not poisonous, to birds, but to prevent dust baths it may be wise to stretch cotton over the area or to lay pea sticks over it.

When your grass comes up weeds may come up as well. Use a weedkiller, such as May and Baker Actrilawn, specially formulated for young grass if they are troublesome. Cut the grass when it is about 2 in (5 cm) high, but cut it no lower than 1 in (2.5 cm). Continue to cut it at about this height; the same applies to new turf. In both cases it is important to keep the grass well watered until it is properly established. A sprinkler is useful for this or, of course, you can put your finger over the end of a hose-pipe to create a fine spray; a watering can will not provide enough water.

Improving a lawn

In most cases you will be faced with an existing lawn that needs improvement – and it is far easier to do this than rip it all up and start again. The problems you will be faced with come under a number of headings.

Weeds A lawn weedkiller will kill most weeds with one or two treatments. If you use a dry, powder type that includes a fertilizer this will stimulate the grass to grow and fill in the gaps left by the dead weeds. Measure and apply it in the same way as grass seed and water it in if no rain falls the next day.

Moss A persistent problem where the lawn stays wet for long periods or is shaded. Try and cut close, collect the grass cuttings and, in especially wet patches, spike the lawn with your fork

every 4 in (10 cm) to help water drain away from the surface. Murphy's Tumblemoss will kill moss quickly and prevent it returning for around six months but this is expensive so use other preventive measures as well.

Thatch Dry grass stems at the base of the grass which gives a very spongy feel to the lawn and encourages moss and diseases. Rake it out with a wire rake or an electric lawn raker.

Wavy edges Do not cut the bulges to match the indents, otherwise your lawn will get smaller and smaller.

1 Cut round and under the indented section with the spade. Turn the turf round and line up the new edge with the old.

2 3 Fill the gap behind it with soil and sow seed in the space. This will soon fill in and the edge will then look straight.

Humps and hollows These problems are treated in similar ways. Cut an 'H' shape in the grass with a spade, with the bar of the 'H' running across the hump or hollow. Undercut with the spade and roll back the grass. ☼ Now either remove a little of the soil or add a little soil as necessary and roll the grass back into position.

General health It is a good idea to feed your lawn every spring and summer with a lawn food suited to that time of year. This will keep it in condition and prevent some of the other problems occurring. If you can go over it with a wire rake every spring and autumn this too will help, but it's hard work and not everyone bothers!

Mowing and edging

The most basic task of all is mowing. To keep a lawn in good condition it may be necessary to mow every week in the peak growing seasons of late spring and

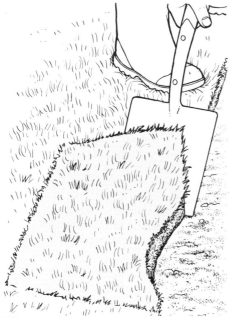

1 Cutting out section with broken edge.

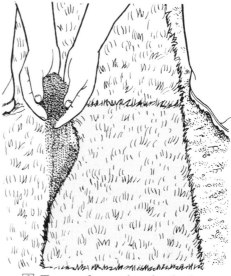

2 Turn turf around so that broken edge is on inside—fill space with soil.

3 Sow grass seed.

☼ Removing excess soil from 'hump' in lawn.

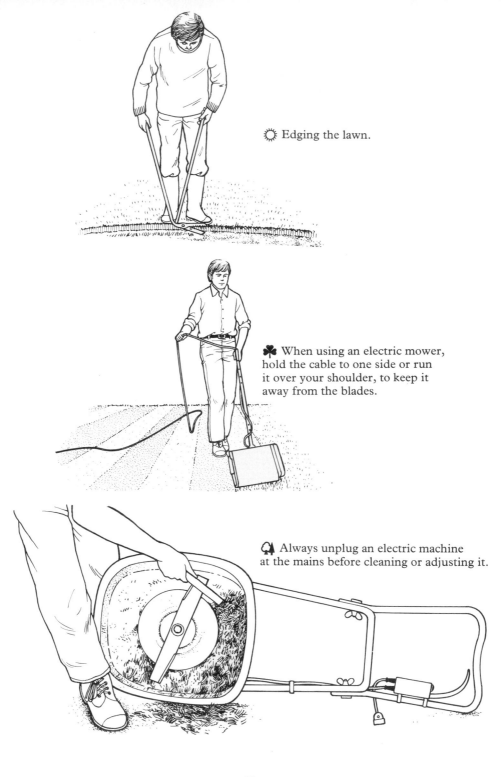

☼ Edging the lawn.

♣ When using an electric mower, hold the cable to one side or run it over your shoulder, to keep it away from the blades.

♧ Always unplug an electric machine at the mains before cleaning or adjusting it.

early autumn. Cutting height varies according to how much the lawn is used. If the children play on it a lot then $\frac{3}{4}$ in (20 cm) is about right but if it gets very little wear then at $\frac{1}{2}$ in (13mm) it will look much better.

In winter you will probably not have to mow at all but in mild spells the grass will start to grow and if it gets longer than about 2 in (5 cm) it is a good idea to take $\frac{1}{2}$–$\frac{3}{4}$ in (13–20 mm) off, otherwise when you come to cut it in the spring it will be so long that you will have a real battle. If you use a hover mower that doesn't have a collection bag try and rake up the cuttings each time you mow. This makes the job longer but it will be good for the grass and help prevent the spread of weeds and moss.

Each time you mow you should cut the edges as well – this improves the look of the lawn immensely. Don't be tempted to use a spade or half-moon lawn edger regularly as you will only reduce the size of the lawn. Edging shears are the most convenient tools or you can get down on your hands and knees with hand shears.

☼ Plastic edging strip laid along the edge of the grass makes edging far easier as there is then no chance of the shears catching the soil. The soil can also be easily thrown away from the edge afterwards so preventing the grass growing out into the bed. Always gather up edge clippings after cutting or you will soon find them taking root.

Special points to remember when using electric mowers
1 Never use them in the rain.
2 Never leave them out in the rain.
3 ✿ Run the cable over your shoulder, or hold it to one side, while mowing, to keep it away from the blades.
4 ♧ Always unplug the machine at the mains before doing any cleaning or adjustment.
5 Never use a hose to clean a machine after use.
6 Never let children play with the mower.

Points to remember about petrol mowers
1 Check whether your machine is four stroke or two stroke. With the former the oil goes in the petrol, with the latter it is separate.
2 Always use the correct mixture in two stroke machines.
3 Check the oil level of four stroke machines before starting the engine and top up if necessary.
4 Never let the machine run out of fuel entirely, top up before the tank is empty.
5 Disconnect the sparking plug before doing any adjustments or changing the height of cut.

One of the easiest ways to brighten up your garden while you get the soil preparation and all the hard work done is to use containers – tubs, troughs, window boxes, hanging baskets, and growing bags that can be positioned on any hard surface.

Tubs

There's a wide range of tubs made of wood, plastic, terra-cotta, reconstituted stone, or compressed wood fibre. The plastic ones are the cheapest but some are rather garish so look around for those that are not too obtrusive – dark green or brown. The wood fibre type fit happily into most gardens but won't last more than a couple of years. Initially tubs are best used for seasonal displays of annuals and bulbs. The few you need can be bought for a reasonable price and will give a dramatic show.

Tubs of annuals or bulbs make very effective focal points when stood in borders. The tubs, raised slightly on

Spring plants for tubs
Crocus
Daffodils
Hyacinths
Pansies
Tulips
Wallflowers

Summer plants for tubs
Antirrhinums
Busy Lizzies
Dwarf dahlias
Fuchsias
Geraniums
Lobelia
Marigolds
Petunias

bricks, should be positioned in a part of the garden which is not at its best when the tub is at *its* prettiest.

The first thing to do when planting your tub is to get it in its final position before you start. If it's for summer, put a tray underneath to help make a water reservoir.

1 Tub planting—pouring in gravel 1 in (2.5 cm) deep.

2 Pour in compost until pot is two-thirds full.

3 Setting the plant in the tub.

4 Filling the remaining space with soil.

1 Now put in some coarse material. Washed stones, pea gravel, or broken clay flower pots are suitable but if you have none of these then just make sure the drainage hole is covered with a piece of perforated zinc so the compost doesn't wash out.

2 Fill the tub two thirds full and firm the compost as you go. Use a John Innes compost, preferably number 2, if you can. A peat based compost will do quite well but drying out in summer can be more of a problem. The best plants for tub use come in pots.

3 Remove the pots and set the plants in the container where they are

5 Water the plant in well.

Aftercare

1 Remove all dead flowers and yellowing leaves as they appear.
2 Water regularly – possibly once a day in summer.
3 Feed every week with a general liquid feed.
4 Look out for pests and diseases, especially greenfly, and treat as necessary.
5 If the tub is near a wall, turn it regularly otherwise all the flowers will be on one side.

to go. As a guide one plant in the centre and four or five round the edge of a tub 12 in (30 cm) across is about right. Set each plant so that the surface of its root ball is 1 in (2.5 cm) below the rim of the tub.

4 5 Fill up with soil firm gently and water in well.

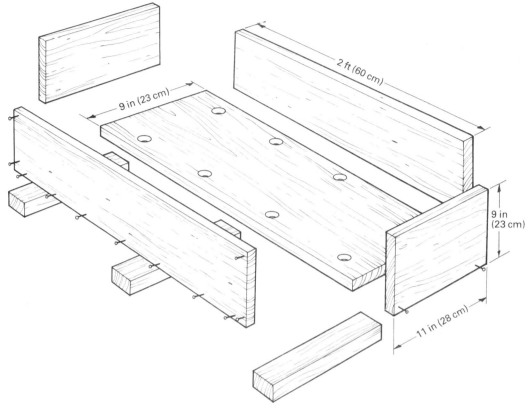

9 in (23 cm)

2 ft (60 cm)

9 in (23 cm)

11 in (28 cm)

☼ Exploded diagram showing construction of 2 ft (60 cm) long window box. The feet, made from 2 × 1 in (5 × 2.5 cm) pieces, may need to be tapered to counteract slope of windowsill.

Window boxes

Window boxes are ideal for bringing extra colour to a small garden. They can be rested on sills if those of your house are large enough, or they can be fixed to the wall below windows – although not, of course, windows that open outwards. Plastic boxes are available in various sizes and you can also now buy sets consisting of a box, tray and bracket.

☼ Alternatively you can make your own timber boxes. This is what you need:

Timber Use elm if you can get it otherwise English whitewood. The size

you need is 9 × 1 in (225 × 25 mm) planed. If you prefer a more rustic finish, go for rough cut timber. For a 2 ft (60 cm) box you'll need 8 ft (2.4 m) of timber.

Nails and screws 2 in (50 cm) brass screws will last the longest but galvanized nails are a good alternative.

Glue A resin-based waterproof wood glue should be used on all joints.

Preservative Use a preservative that is safe with plants, usually the green or red cedar finish, and not creosote. If you want to paint over the preservative, use aluminium primer after the preservative for pale colours or ordinary wood primer for dark ones plus under-coat and top coat. Give all the cut and drilled timber two treatments of preservative before fixing together.

Tools Saw, set square, hammer, pencil, drill, $\frac{1}{12}$ in (2 mm) bit and $1\frac{1}{4}$ in (3 cm) bit, brush for preservative, jar for glue mixing and stick to spread it plus, ideally, a pair of rubber gloves.

Mount the box using steel brackets fixed with Rawlplugs and long screws.

Lay some perforated zinc or fine plastic mesh in the bottom to stop the compost falling through the holes, then two thirds fill with compost; either a soil-less or John Innes type. Set the plants in position, top up and firm well. Finish off with a good watering. Do all this with the box in position.

Plants for window boxes – spring
Crocus
Daisies
Daffodils
Dwarf wallflowers
Forget-me-nots
Grape hyacinths
Hyacinths
Pansies
Polyanthus
Tulips

Plants for window boxes – summer
Ageratum
Antirrhinums
Begonias
Busy Lizzies
Dianthus
Fuchsias
Gazanias
Geraniums
Lobelia
Marigolds
Petunia

Make sure that you dead-head regularly (snip off faded blooms) to keep up a constant supply of good flowers, and check for pests and diseases, too. If you come across any, treat them at once with the right chemical. Watering is very important, especially later in the season when the box gets crowded. And don't forget to feed, too. Either use a weekly liquid feed or fertilizer spikes.

Permanent plants are less successful in boxes because they tend to get rather large and they are usually only at their best for a short period – for the rest of the time the box will not be very attractive. Use them as a skeleton if you like – planting seasonal bloomers around them. Good plants to try are ivies, variegated hebes, euonymus and other dwarf evergreens.

Hanging baskets
Every garden has space for at least one hanging basket. Even if you live in a flat you can hang one outside a window.

There are a number of types on the market. The wire basket is the traditional type and the soil is kept in place using moss or a basket liner. If you use moss, line the basket with polythene as well otherwise, if the birds steal your moss, all the soil will fall out. There are also plastic baskets available and in many ways these are easier to manage. They dry out less quickly and many have a built-in water reservoir to make the chore of watering less frequent.

If you are buying a plastic basket look out for those with holes in the side. Most do not have this facility but by planting through the sides you will create an attractive basket much more quickly.

Watering is the one problem that everyone has with baskets; they dry out

Planting a hanging basket

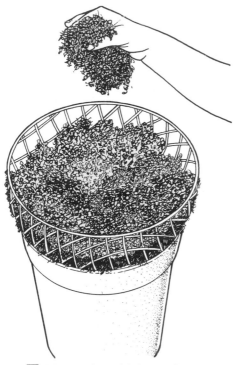

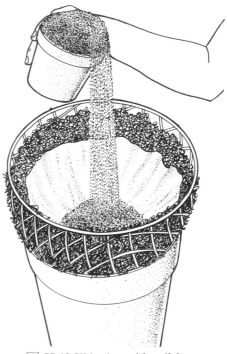

☐1 Line basket with layer of moss.

☐2 Half-fill basket with soil-less potting compost.

quickly. By mid-summer they are full of plants and use a lot of water. What's more, as they tend to hang by sunny walls, the heat that the walls reflect makes them dry out even more. So anything that you can do to keep them moist is worthwhile. Watering twice a day may well be necessary in summer.

Planting

☐1 Stand your basket on a larger flower pot or bucket to keep it stable. First of all line it with a thick layer of moss, say about 1 in (2.5 cm). Carpet underlay is a good cheap alternative. Then line it with a layer of medium grade polythene and poke a few holes in the bottom. Make a water reservoir by sitting a saucer on the bottom and filling it with pea gravel or washed stones from the garden.

☐2 Now half fill with soil-less potting compost. Make some holes through the sides and slide a plant through each hole then carry on filling with compost until the basket is almost full.

☐3 Now put in the last plants and top up with soil. Water thoroughly.

☐4 Screw a bracket in place on the wall high enough so that people won't hit their heads on the basket when it's in place, then hang the basket up.

The easiest way to water is with a hosepipe. Tie a length of hose to a 4 ft (1.2 m) cane with 9 in (23 cm) projecting at one end and put a hose connector on the other. This can be connected to the mains and the basket watered by simply holding the cane with the water

3 Putting in the last plants.

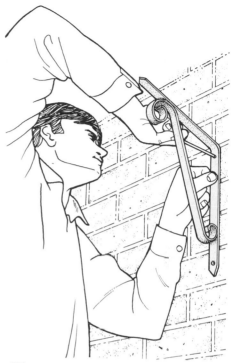

4 Make sure the bracket is fixed firmly.

dribbling into the basket – it saves tottering on a chair with a can. During the summer turn the basket occasionally otherwise all the plants will grow away from the wall.

Most of the summer plants which do well in window boxes also do well in baskets but it is a good idea not to choose the taller types of marigolds and antirrhinums. One bushy plant in the centre is enough and it's probably best that the others be floppy. Busy Lizzies are best if the basket is going to be shaded for most of the day. Again watering and feeding are crucial so get a neighbour to look after your basket when you're on holiday.

It will help if the baskets are un-hooked and stood on large flower pots in a shady and sheltered part of the garden while you are away. They will then dry out more slowly and cause the neighbours less trouble.

For a spring display the range is much restricted, pansies are probably the most successful plants although crocus and forget-me-nots are sometimes used very effectively.

You can also grow perennial plants in baskets. The best plants for growing in this way are probably the ornamental ivies – the sort that are often grown as house plants. These are hardy in all but the coldest parts of the country and a basket of them makes an attractive feature in a porch or outside a front door.

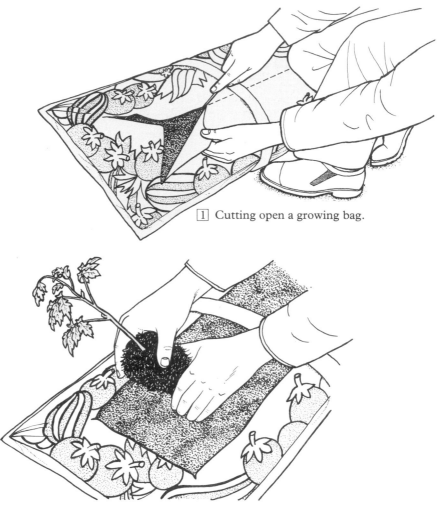

1 Cutting open a growing bag.

2 Planting along the centre line of the bag.

Growing bags

The introduction of growing bags has revolutionized tomato growing and growing in containers generally. They are, quite simply, polythene bolsters of peat, peat and sand, or peat and bark, with the addition of a fertilizer to help sustain the plants for their first few weeks. Although they are mainly used for tomatoes they are also suitable for peppers, aubergines and cucumbers, plus hardy vegetables like lettuce, beetroot, spring onions and beans. Strawberries do very well in growing bags and there are any number of bedding plants and bulbs which will also succeed. Only perennial plants are unsuited to them.

Tomatoes Put no more than three plants in each bag.

☼ For bedding plants, mix upright ones with sprawlers.

♣ Newspaper test for moisture content.

1 Get the bag in position in a greenhouse or at the base of a sunny wall, and cut it open into two long rectangles. Loosen the peat if it appears to be compacted and water it if it seems very dry.

2 Knock the plants out of their pots and plant them as evenly as possible along the centre of the bag. To stake them special supports are available for holding bamboo canes.

Cucumbers Two plants only per bag are sufficient. In a greenhouse tie pea and bean netting to the bag and to the roof as a support and use greenhouse varieties of cucumber. Outside, use outdoor varieties and let them sprawl.

Peppers Only three plants per bag in a greenhouse or sunny spot outside.

Aubergines Three plants per bag; best grown in a greenhouse.

Strawberries Six to eight plants per bag are about right. For an early crop slide the bag on to a board and move it into a cold greenhouse before Christmas.

☼ **Bedding** Try and choose some upright types like antirrhinums together with sprawlers such as petunias.

For spring, try tulips and pansies.

♣ Looking after growing bags is not always as easy as it seems, particularly as it can be difficult to tell when they need water. The simplest test is to press a piece of newspaper on to the peat. If it picks up water the bag is moist enough, if not, a drink is needed.

At the height of the summer tomatoes in a greenhouse may need watering twice a day. To make this easier to cope with there are water reservoirs available which go under the bag. Wicks pushed into the bottom of the bag take water from the tray into the peat. There is usually enough water in a full tray to last two or three days in summer and rather more at other times.

Feeding is vital. Indeed it is not a bad idea to water the plants in with a weak solution of liquid feed when planting. Then for summer plants, a feed every week or ten days is necessary as there are only limited supplies in the bag. Use a tomato feed for tomatoes, peppers, aubergines, cucumbers and strawberries and a general feed for other plants. For spring plants the fertilizer in the bag is usually sufficient.

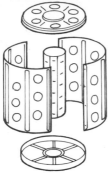

[1] Construction of strawberry barrel.

[2] Start to fill with compost.

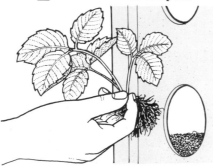

[3] Inserting a strawberry plant through hole in side.

☼ Central tube allows water to reach bottom.

Fruit and vegetables

The range of food crops that can be grown in containers is wide but some are easier to cope with than others. The crops suggested for growing bags are not difficult and can also be grown in other containers.

Some fruit trees can be grown in large tubs and if you have little space this is a good idea. There are two important provisos. Use as large a container as possible and buy a tree on a dwarfing rootstock. This means that the apple variety has been grafted on to special roots which keep it dwarf and encourage early fruiting.

Some herbs such as chives, rosemary, thyme, parsley tarragon and mint do well in containers too.

Strawberries are ideal container plants and this fact has been capitalized upon by the introduction of strawberry barrels. These cylindrical plastic barrels are filled with compost and strawberries are set in the top and through holes in the sides. Some even have a base on which the barrel rotates so all the plants can get some sunshine.

[1] Assemble the barrel in the position where it is to stay.

[2] Start to fill with compost firming as you go.

[3] As you come to holes in the sides, slide the plants through, roots first from outside to inside and then carry on filling and planting until you come to the top. Put the last plants in the top.

☼ Some barrels have a central tube for watering and this is very useful as it helps ensure that water reaches the bottom of the barrel. Like plants in other containers, they will need feeding regularly. A tomato feed is suitable.

Raised beds

These are really no more than large permanent containers. They can be made of ornamental stone or concrete blocks, even old railway sleepers and of bricks. One of the simplest arrangements is to make the walls dry using bricks and polythene sheeting.

1 Mark out the area the bed is to cover and lay down the first row of bricks. Fork over the area in between, remove any weeds, and tread the soil well; then continue to add another two courses of bricks, bonding them as you would any wall. The bricks you use should be hard, frost-resistant types not those, usually called Flettons, which cannot stand frost.

2 After three courses line the bed with polythene sheeting – old peat sacks are ideal – and make some holes in the base with a knife. Then put in 3 in (7.5 cm) of rubble, stones, etc. for drainage. Lay the polythene on the top row of bricks and then add the last course. Make sure that the polythene is tucked well into corners.

3 Spread a layer of sacking over the rubble to prevent the compost from washing through and then fill up with compost. You can use a soil-based John Innes mixture from the garden centre, choose No. 2, or mix your own using three parts of good garden soil, one part peat and one sharp sand.

If you want to grow plants that enjoy acid soil (p. 10), buy a special 'ericaclous' mixture or for rock plants add an extra part of sand.

4 Fill the box, firming as you go and then put the plants in and water them well. Don't forget to plant trailers to hang down the sides.

1 Laying the first course of bricks.

2 Lining the bed with polythene sheeting.

3 Filling the bed with compost.

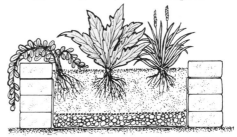

4 Sectional view of planted bed.

Every plant in your garden is vulnerable to pest and disease attack. It sounds depressing but fortunately there is a lot that you can do to prevent minor troubles and avoid the necessity of using chemical sprays; however safe they may be, the fewer we use the better. A lot of careful research goes into the testing of garden chemicals and only those which are least likely to cause problems are approved. Nevertheless it pays to try and make sure that plants never get to the stage where chemicals are needed. Plants which are healthy and growing well are more able to resist attack, or to ride it out if they do suffer.

Remember these guidelines

1 Prepare the soil well before planting, using adequate organic matter.
2 Feed regularly to keep plants growing well.
3 Don't over feed as this can make plants vulnerable.
4 Water thoroughly in dry spells.
5 Put plants in soil that suits them.
6 Choose disease-resistant varieties if possible.
7 Look at plants carefully before buying and reject anything substandard.
8 Rotate vegetable crops (p. 38) to prevent disease build up.
9 Keep the garden tidy and clear up all dead leaves.
10 Keep the garden weed free – weeds can harbour pests and diseases.
11 Check plants regularly and pick off by hand any parts which are infected.
12 Avoid damaging plants by careless hoeing, loose ties, and wayward mowing.

Fruit problems

Red spider mite
Apples, peaches, nectarines and especially strawberries
Leaves loose their lustre and whitish or yellow patches appear which turn bronze. Some web-like strands may be seen around leaves. Minute mites are sometimes visible on undersides of leaves.
Use Murphy's Liquid Derris or Boots Greenfly killer.

☼ Raspberry beetle
Raspberries, loganberries, blackberries and other cane fruits
Fruits eaten by maggots.
Use Murphy's Liquid Derris or ICI Picket when the first flowers open and again when the fruits start to turn pink.

Silverleaf
Cherries, plums and gages
Silvery speckling of foliage, usually on one part of the tree. Infected wood stained brown inside.
Cut out infected branches to 1 ft (30 cm) below stain. Paint wounds with May and Baker Seal and Heal.

Scab
Apples and pears
Small rough brown patches on fruits. Spray with ICI Nimrod T or pbi Benlate every fortnight from when the leaves first appear until July.

❧ Brown rot
Apples, pears, plums
Fruits go soft and brown on the tree, on the ground or in storage. Rings of white 'wax' appear later. Remove affected fruit from tree and burn, store only undamaged fruit, clear windfalls, store fruit so it does not touch.

Canker
Tree fruits

Causes rough sunken areas on branches of apples and pears and die back of shoots. Plums and cherries also ooze gum.

Cut out infected areas if the damage is slight, otherwise remove entire branches and paint wounds with May and Baker Seal and Heal.

♣ *Big bud mite*
Blackcurrants

Buds unusually round and fat in winter. Caused by a mite which also spreads reversion virus, this causing a dramatic reduction in cropping. Usually most common in old and neglected bushes.

Pick off big buds, if many buds are infected dig up and burn the bush.

Virus
Soft fruits

Various symptoms including stunting of growth, loss of yield, and twisted and misshapen leaves.

Dig up and burn infected plants. Renew strawberries every four years. Keep down greenfly which spread viruses. Don't replant new stock on sites from which infected ones have been removed.

○ Maggot of raspberry beetle.

❀ Brown rot on apple.

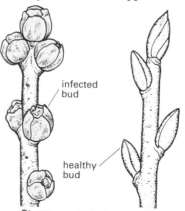

infected bud

healthy bud

♣ Effect of big bud mite on blackcurrant.

Flower problems

☼ **Aphids** *(Blackfly, greenfly and various other shades)*
Attack most plants, particularly buds and soft young tips
Spray deciduous shrubs and fruit with Murphy Mortegg in winter. Treat infections with ICI Rapid or Abol G as they appear.

Earwigs
Chrysanthemums, dahlias and zinnias
Eat buds and petals during the night. Put upturned flower pots full of straw on canes amongst plants and burn contents every morning. Alternatively spray with Murphy Lindex Garden Spray.

🍀 **Thrips** *(Thunderflies)*
Gladioli, chrysanths, iris, montbretia, dahlia
Tiny insects causing fine yellow or silvery mottling and bleaching. Also carry viruses. Spray with Murphy's Liquid Derris or Boots Greenfly Killer at the first sign.

Leaf Miner
Chrysanthemum, cineraria, holly
Blistered tunnels under upper surface of the leaves.
Spray with Murphy Lindex Garden Spray or ICI Sybol 2 at the first sign. Also attacks groundsel so control this weed.

🌲 **Mildew**
Roses, Michaelmas daisies, calendula and many others
White felt over young flower buds and young foliage.
Spray with Murphy Tumblelite or ICI Nimrod T every two weeks.

Botrytis
Many plants
Soft rotting areas covered with grey mould.
Pick off small infected areas otherwise spray with May and Baker Fungus Fighter and remove dead flowers and leaves – infection often starts here.

Rusts
Roses, antirrhinum, hollyhock, geraniums
Rusty brown spots and sometimes streaks on foliage and stems.
Spray with Murphy Tumbleblite.

❊ **Blackspot**
Roses
Black spots on foliage which merge as the leaf turns yellow. Leaves drop and bush deteriorates. Can kill bushes entirely. Starts low down and spreads up the plants.
Pick off infected leaves, spray bad attacks with Murphy Tumbleblite.

Virus
Many plants especially border plants
Variety of symptoms including stunting, poor flower development, flecks or streaks of contrasting colours in flowers, unusual leaf characteristics (twisting, brittle feel, sharply toothed edges). Dig up and burn infected plants. Control aphids which spread viruses.

Wilt
Paeonies and clematis
Sudden collapse of stems or whole plants. On paeonies, buds rot.
Cut off and burn infected shoots and drench foliage and soil with pbi Benlate or May and Baker Fungus Fighter.

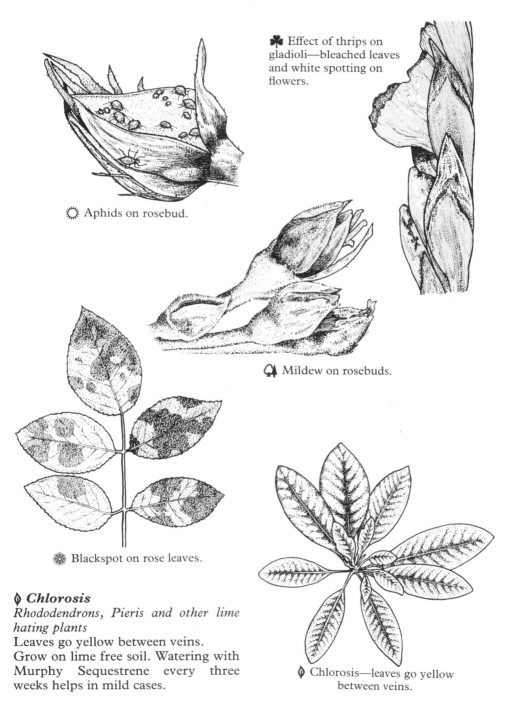

✿ Effect of thrips on gladioli—bleached leaves and white spotting on flowers.

☼ Aphids on rosebud.

♧ Mildew on rosebuds.

❋ Blackspot on rose leaves.

◊ *Chlorosis*
Rhododendrons, Pieris and other lime hating plants
Leaves go yellow between veins.
Grow on lime free soil. Watering with Murphy Sequestrene every three weeks helps in mild cases.

◊ Chlorosis—leaves go yellow between veins.

Vegetable problems

Slugs
Seedlings and soft foliage of many crops
Seedlings eaten off at ground level, holes in foliage of lettuce, cabbage etc. Slime trails visible.
pbi Slug Gard or May and Baker Slug Trap.

☼ Root flies
Carrot, cabbage, onion
Maggots eating roots. Cabbages turn blue and plants collapse, carrot foliage turns red, onion leaves go yellow and wilt.
Use May and Baker Soil Insecticide or pbi Bromophos in drills when sowing. Protect transplanted cabbages with root collars.

Pigeons
Cabbage family, peas
Foliage eaten often leaving veins.
Cover with pigeon netting.

Eelworm
Potatoes
Leaves shrivel, small nodules found on roots, plants stunted, very small crops. Dig up and burn plants, keep potatoes off the area for at least eight years. Rotate crops.

♣ Caterpillars
Cabbage family
Irregular holes in leaves.
Pick off caterpillars, or spray with Murphy Tumblebug or ICI Picket.

♧ Blight
Potatoes and tomatoes
Leaves go yellow then brown and fold downwards from the tip back. Prevalent after muggy weather.
Spray as a precaution with Murphy Liquid Copper or pbi Dithane every two weeks from mid-summer.

❀ Clubroot
Cabbage family
Plants stunted and weak. Roots swollen, distorted and smelly.
Apply lime before planting. Dip plants in Murphy Clubroot Dip when planting. Rotate crops on a longer rotation.

Scab
Potatoes
Small brown scabs on tubers. No leaf symptoms.
Use more organic matter before planting, water well and avoid liming in the year or two before planting.

◊ Bolting
Lettuce, spinach and other leaf crops, plus leeks and onions
Tall flowering stems emerge from the head of plant.
In leaf crops usually due to hot dry weather and not harvesting when crops are at their prime. Inferior onion sets sometimes bolt and leeks can do so in the spring.

Root splitting
Root crops
Vertical splits in root.
Usually the result of a sudden wet spell after drought. The plant suddenly grows quickly and the skin splits. Water well in dry spells to keep crops growing.

Virus
Peas, potatoes, marrows and courgettes, swede and turnip
Distortion of foliage, stunted growth, leaves mottled yellow.
Dig up and burn infected plants. Control aphids.

Vegetable problems

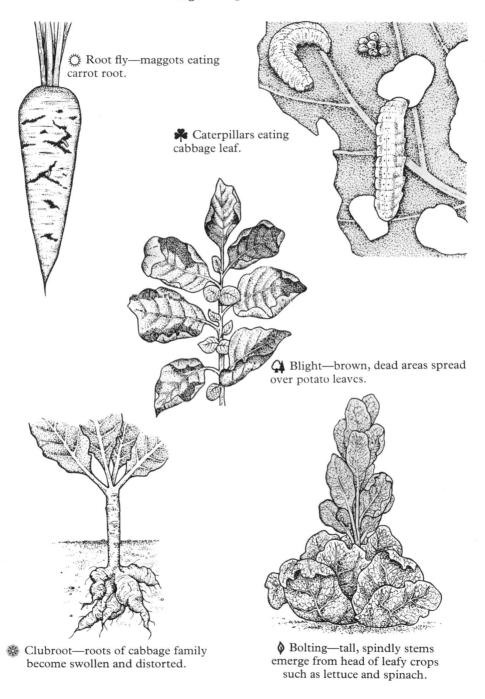

☼ Root fly—maggots eating carrot root.

☘ Caterpillars eating cabbage leaf.

♧ Blight—brown, dead areas spread over potato leaves.

❀ Clubroot—roots of cabbage family become swollen and distorted.

♦ Bolting—tall, spindly stems emerge from head of leafy crops such as lettuce and spinach.

Greenhouse and house plant problems

☼ *Red spider mite*
Many plants
Yellow speckling of leaves and weblike strands around foliage.
Can build up unnoticed as it is unobtrusive in its early stages.
Keep atmosphere moist. Spray with Murphy Liquid Derris, Murphy Tumblebug or ICI Sybol 2.

❋ *Mealy bug*
Many long lived plants and not usually annuals
Tiny oval creatures covered in a white, wax like substance. Colonies tend to be surrounded by white fluff. Paint isolated colonies with methylated spirits or Boots Greenfly Killer. Fumigate greenhouses with Fumite Insecticide Smoke or spray with Murphy Tumblebug.

Scale insect
Many plants though not usually annuals
Brownish oval scales in isolation or in colonies on stems, leaf stalks, midribs. Spray with Bio Flydown, Murphy Greenhouse Aerosol or Boots Greenfly Killer.

🐛 *White fly*
Tomatoes, cinerarias and many other greenhouse and house plants
Small pure white flies which hide under leaves but fly around when disturbed.
Use Synchemicals House Plant Pest Killer, ICI Picket, Murphy Tumblebug, or pbi Longlast.

❀ *Damping off*
Seedlings
Seedlings collapse in seed trays or after pricking out.
Sow seeds thinly. Avoid damaging seedlings when pricking out. Use clean pots and trays and proprietary compost. Don't overwater. Remove glass or polythene covering on trays as soon as seedlings germinate. Water with pbi Cheshunt Compound or Murphy Liquid Copper Fungicide.

Blossom End Rot
Tomatoes
Opposite end of fruit from stalk goes dark brown or black.
Usually caused by plants drying out so keep them well watered, especially when fruits are ripening.

Botrytis
Many greenhouse plants
Leaves go yellow and collapse, then grow a grey mould. Also affects flowers; collect up dead flowers and leaves and remove them from the greenhouse. Ventilate well and spray with Murphy Systemic Fungicide or pbi Benlate.

◊ *Sooty mould*
Many plants
Black sooty growth on upper surface of leaves. Grow on the honeydew which drops from aphids, whitefly, scale insects etc., feeding on the undersides of the leaves above.
Control these pests and wipe mould off with a cloth.

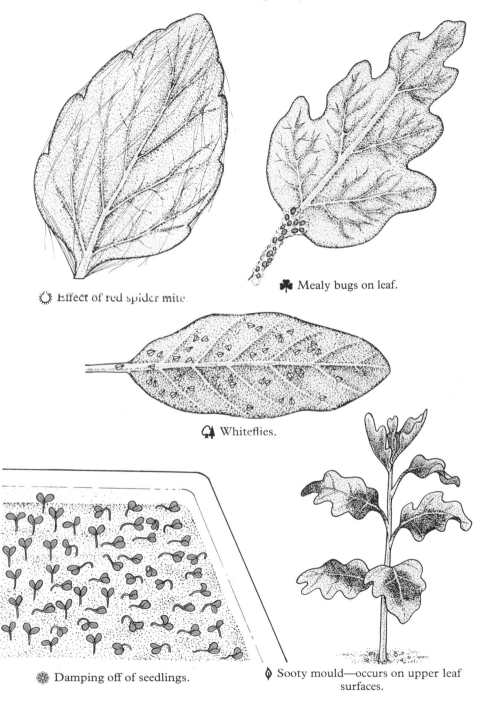

Effect of red spider mite.

Mealy bugs on leaf.

Whiteflies.

Damping off of seedlings.

Sooty mould—occurs on upper leaf surfaces.

Pests and disease control

Apart from the preventative measures described on p. 80 and some of the specific measures mentioned in the past few pages, most control measures are based on chemicals.

These come in the form of liquids, powders or granules to mix with water, dusts, fumigants, pellets, aerosols and cardboard pins.

Liquids The cap is usually used as a measure to make up the spray. Some measures make up large quantities which can be wasteful. Put the chemical in the sprayer first, then the water.

Powders Packed in sachets with measured amounts.

1 Mix them with a little water.
2 Tip the liquid into the sprayer.
3 Rinse out the bowl into the sprayer and top up to the correct level with water.

Granules Again in measured sachets usually for one pint or one gallon of spray. They dissolve well without pre-mixing with water.

Dusts Packed in soft canisters for puffing on the affected areas of the plants. Can be difficult to apply evenly and they look unsightly.

Fumigants For greenhouses only. Pellets or cones are lit with a match and the greenhouse fills with chemical smoke. Very effective and penetrates every corner. Use in the evening after a warm day, ventilate well in the morning before going inside.

Aerosols Very useful for treating small attacks especially in the greenhouse. Expensive but convenient.

Pellets For killing slugs. Modern pellets are used very sparingly, one per plant or every 6 in (15 cm), and are unlikely to harm pets unless the packet itself is raided. Those containing methiocarb are safest.

Cardboard pins Intended for house plants, these are pushed into the soil in the pots, the pesticide is released and taken up by plants. Very useful indoors where you don't really want to use sprays.

Having made up a spray, make sure you use it safely and effectively.

Care with chemicals

1 Never use more or less than the makers recommend.
2 Stop spraying just before the liquid starts to run off the foliage.
3 ☼ Try to cover the stems and undersides of leaves as well as the upper surfaces.
4 Wear rubber gloves and keep sleeves rolled down while spraying. Never breathe in spray.
5 Do not use the same sprayer for pesticides and weedkillers. Use separate ones and keep them labelled.
6 Do not spray open flowers.
7 Do not spray on windy days.
8 Store all chemicals in their original containers – **do not decant them into other bottles** – and keep them out of children's reach.
9 Wash well after use and rinse out containers down a drain or flush down the lavatory.
10 Read the instructions on the packet carefully before buying and before spraying and follow them precisely.

Care with chemicals

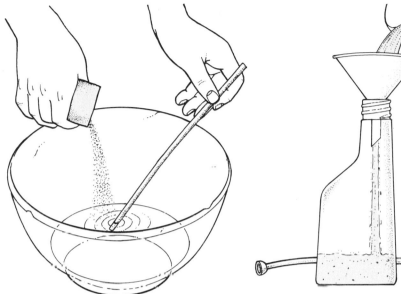

1 Mix the powder with a little water.

2 Pour mixed solution into sprayer.

3 Rinse out the bowl.

☼ When spraying, try to ensure coverage of stems and undersides of leaves.

Weeds

The weed problem is one which is never entirely absent from any garden. No matter what you do, seeds are going to blow in from next door or roots are going to creep in under the fence. What's more, with an average of 20,000 viable weed seeds in every square yard of soil waiting to germinate, the problem is going to take some time to lessen, no matter what we do.

There's quite an array of chemicals to deal with them but there are also a number of ways of keeping them under control without using chemicals. Whichever method of weed control you choose, the sooner you put it into effect the better, before more weed seeds are shed.

Hoeing Hoeing regularly will kill weed seedlings almost before they appear and also weaken tougher weeds with large roots deep in the soil.

☼ Some· weeds, such as annual meadow grass, take root again very easily.

Planting By growing plants so that they make a dense carpet over the soil most weeds will be smothered.

Mulching A layer of organic matter such as peat or compost over the surface of the soil will prevent weeds getting established or coming through from down below.

Hand pulling Just keeping your eyes open while you're walking round the garden and pulling out any offenders will be very helpful.

Preventing spread Never let any weed to to seed and when digging never leave any roots in the soil.

However, in many cases chemicals are necessary. There are a number of different types and ways of putting them on:

Weed preventers These are chemicals such as Murphy Covershield, Syn-chemicals Casaron G and Murphy Weedex which are put on the soil after weeds have been cleared and which prevent weed seeds coming up.

♣ They do not prevent weeds like couch grass sending up shoots from roots under the soil nor do they kill existing weeds. They vary in their persistence and can be used on all areas of the garden though there are certain restrictions as to the plants which are safe to treat.

Weedex is especially useful on paths and gravel drives where it will keep weeds at bay for at least six months, Casaron G in shrub beds and borders and Covershield in the vegetable garden and amongst bedding.

Contact weedkillers These are weedkillers which kill foliage but nothing else. ICI Weedol is the best known.

♧ It will burn off all green parts of a plant and for annual weeds such as groundsel this is quite sufficient to kill.

❀ Weeds like couch grass and bindweed, with fat underground roots, will shoot again from below ground level.

This weedkiller is very poisonous so special care should be taken when using it. If any spray reaches the leaves of your flowers they will be killed too, although a few spots will do little harm to the plant as a whole.

Weeds

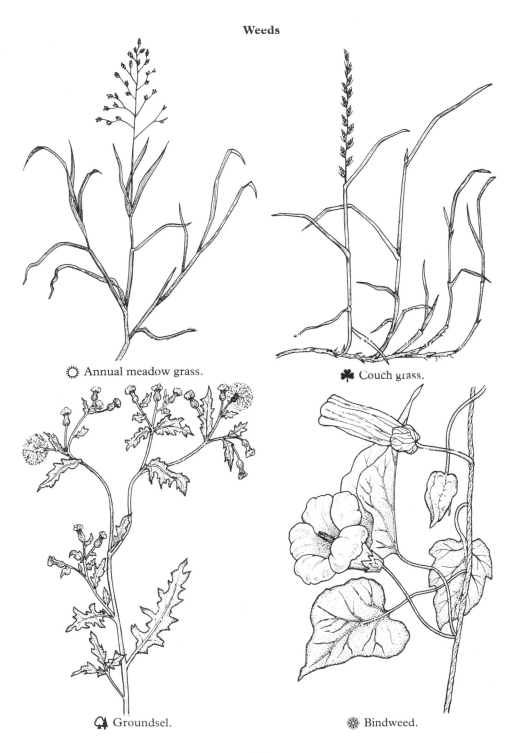

☼ Annual meadow grass.

☘ Couch grass.

♧ Groundsel.

✺ Bindweed.

Translocated ('hormone') weed-killers These are sprayed or watered on to the leaves of the weeds, are absorbed into the plants, taken right down into the roots and kill the weeds from the inside. Murphy's Tumbleweed, May and Baker Weed Out and ICI Verdone are examples. These will all kill the more difficult types of weeds which usually shoot again from the roots.

☼ It's useful to be able to recognize the different nettles. Contact weed-killer will kill the annual type, translocated weedkiller is needed for the perennial type.

Just to confuse the issue, weedkillers can be divided in a different way into total weedkillers and selective weed-killers. As the name implies total weed-killers affect all weeds, and indeed all plants, while selective weedkillers affect some and not others.

Total weedkillers Examples are ICI Weedol and Murphy's Tumbleweed. They will affect any plants on to which they are applied, and so special care must be taken. They must only be used where you really do want to kill everything. Weedol will kill all annual and young perennial weeds; Tumbleweed will kill everything.

Selective weedkillers The best examples are lawn weedkillers, such as ICI Verdone – this will kill the weeds in grass but not the grass itself. May and Baker Weed Out is rather different in that it can be sprayed on to flower borders in spring and summer but will only kill the couch grass growing between the flowers; the flowers themselves will be unharmed.

Problem weeds There are some weeds which are particularly difficult to control.

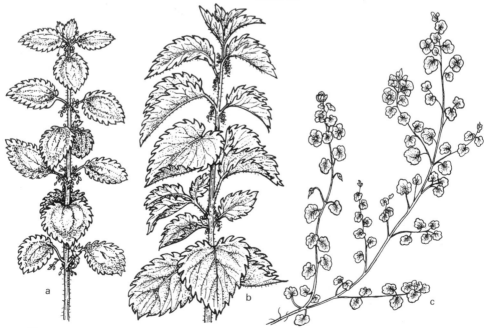

☼ (*a*) Annual nettle (*Urtica urens*), (*b*) Common (perennial) nettle (*Urtica dioica*), ♣ (*c*) Speedwell.

❀ Using a dribble bar ensures an even application of weedkiller.

♣ Speedwell in lawns is a good example. Most lawn weedkillers will not touch it so you have to be very specific in the one you choose. In this case use May and Baker Actrilawn.

♧ Particularly persistent weeds like horsetail can also be difficult to banish and here only Murphy's Tumbleweed will have any effect and it may need two or three treatments.

❀ The technique of application is important. On lawns and paths it's vital to get an even application and the best approach is to use a dribble bar on a watering can. Application close to borders is also easy. If you need to apply chemicals around plants a hood on a sprayer is the most convenient method as it prevents any drift.

On a lawn, a simple way to ensure even application is to divide it into measured areas so that the recom-mended amount of chemical can be applied. If you are using a weedkiller that comes as a dry powder, the lawn can be divided into square yards using canes or strings and a measured amount sprinkled on each square yard.

Weeds growing amongst flowers need very careful treatment. Murphy Tumbleweed comes in a gel with a brush in the lid of the bottle so it can be painted on the weed leaves. This can also be used where you have just one or two weeds needing attention.

On lawns where there may only be a few weeds, aerosol spot weeders are available from which you squirt a weedkiller foam directly on to the weed.

Aerosol spot weeders are also available for the treatment of isolated weeds in paths and these are also useful in borders.

INDEX